READY
STEADY
COOK
3

READY STEADY COOK 3

KEVIN WOODFORD

LESLEY WATERS

PHOTOGRAPHS BY
JULIET PIDDINGTON

BBC BOOKS

This book is published to accompany the television series *Ready Steady Cook*
which was first broadcast in Autumn 1994.
The series was produced by Bazal Productions.

Published by BBC Books, an imprint of BBC Worldwide Publishing,
BBC Worldwide Ltd, Woodlands, 80 Wood Lane, London W12 0TT.

First published 1997
Format © Bazal Productions
Recipes © Kevin Woodford and Lesley Waters
The moral right of the authors has been asserted
Photographs: Juliet Piddington
Home Economist: Sarah Ramsbottom
ISBN 0 563 38324 0

Set in Futura
Designed by Louise Morley
Printed by Martins the Printers Ltd, Berwick-upon-Tweed
Bound by Hunter & Foulis Ltd, Edinburgh
Colour separation by Radstock Reproductions Ltd, Midsomer Norton
Colour printing by Lawrence Allen Ltd, Weston-super-Mare
Cover printed by Belmont Press, Northampton

CONTENTS

INTRODUCTION

People are always asking me if the chefs on **Ready Steady Cook** actually know in advance what's in those mystery bags. I can honestly answer no, they are a complete surprise. The contestants choose their combination of foods carefully and our talented chefs really do have to create a culinary masterpiece on the spot within the all-important 20-minute time limit.

We know you like to try the delicious recipes you see on the screen. So, to save you scribbling away in front of the telly, we have put together another selection of some of our favourite dishes from the show. We've also put in plenty of those handy hints that can turn just another routine weekday supper into a gourmet feast.

Now all you have to do is pick a recipe, raid your larder and prepare yourself to **Ready Steady Cook**!

[signature]

x

Presenter, **Ready Steady Cook**

A Note on Ingredients and Techniques

Good-quality ingredients make all the difference to the taste of the finished dish. For best results, choose unsalted butter and extra virgin olive oil. Buy ripe, flavoursome tomatoes, and whenever possible, really fresh herbs. If a recipe specifies dried herbs, freeze-dried ones usually have the best flavour. For desserts, chocolate should contain at least 50 per cent cocoa solids – check the back of the wrapper.

Some of the recipes contain raw or lightly cooked eggs. Because of the slight risk of salmonella poisoning, these should be avoided by the sick, the elderly, the very young, and pregnant women.
The chances of contamination are greatly reduced if you buy free-range eggs, preferably organic, from a reputable supplier.

Many of the recipes in this book include wine. Use a wine that you would enjoy drinking rather than cheap 'cooking' wine – if it's not worth drinking it's not worth cooking with! You can use unsweetened apple juice or stock if you prefer.

The chefs on **Ready Steady Cook** often cook on a ridged grill pan. Ridged grill pans are made of cast iron and usually have a spout for pouring off the cooking juices. They are a very healthy way of cooking because the ridges keep the food raised above any fat that runs off. They also make attractive grill marks on food – to make a criss-cross pattern, give the food a half-turn half way through cooking each side. Use ridged grill pans for steaks, chops, fish or chunky slices of vegetables such as aubergines, courgettes or peppers.

Finally, **Ready Steady Cook** is all about putting together a delicious meal from whatever ingredients you have to hand. The recipes in this book are proof that some of the most memorable dishes are the ones that come about on the spur of the moment. So, if you don't have a particular ingredient, follow the example of our chefs and improvise. Don't be afraid to get in the kitchen and **Ready Steady Cook!**

LARDER INGREDIENTS USED ON
READY STEADY COOK

Arrowroot
Baking powder
Balsamic vinegar
Bay leaves
Beef stock cubes
Bottle of red wine
Bottle of white wine
Caster sugar
Cayenne pepper
Chicken stock cubes
Chilli powder
Cornflour
Demerara sugar
Dijon mustard
Double cream
Dried mixed herbs
Dried oregano
Eggs, size 3
Fresh basil
Fresh coriander
Fresh dill
Fresh parsley
Fresh rosemary
Fresh sage
Fresh thyme
Fresh white bread
Garam masala
Garlic

Golden syrup
Granulated sugar
Greek yoghurt
Ground all-spice
Ground cinnamon
Ground coriander
Ground ginger
Ground nutmeg
Honey
Lemons/Limes
Milk
Olive oil
Oranges
Plain flour
Red-wine vinegar
Self-raising flour
Sesame oil
Soft brown sugar
Soy sauce
Sunflower oil
Tabasco sauce
Tomato purée
Tomato sauce
Turmeric
Unsalted butter
Vegetable stock cubes
White-wine vinegar
Wholegrain mustard

VEGETARIAN DISHES

LESLEY WATERS

VEGGIES FOR VISHNU

Vegetable *tarte tatin* with tomato relish and vegetable fritters

Indira Ragubeer had only been in the UK for a year and was facing two problems. One was the cold weather and the other was her husband, Vishnu, who hated vegetables. Although Lesley managed to create something to change Vishnu's opinion of veggies, she couldn't help with changing the weather!

SERVES 2
FOR THE *TARTE TATIN*
Olive oil
1 large red pepper, seeded and sliced
1 large courgette, sliced
$1/_2$ red onion, finely chopped
1 tablespoon chopped fresh parsley
225 g (8 oz) ready-to-roll shortcrust pastry
Salt and freshly ground black pepper

FOR THE RELISH
5 tomatoes, roughly chopped
2 garlic cloves, chopped

2 tablespoons chopped fresh coriander
$1/_2$ red onion, finely chopped
Salt and freshly ground black pepper

FOR THE FRITTERS
Sunflower oil, for deep-frying
3 eggs, beaten
Plain flour
1 aubergine, sliced
1 courgette, sliced
Salt and freshly ground black pepper

Pre-heat the oven to gas mark 6, 200°C, 400°F. To make the vegetable *tarte tatin*, heat 2 tablespoons of the olive oil in a 23-cm frying-pan that you can also use in the oven (or use an ordinary frying pan and transfer to a loose bottomed cake tin after frying). Arrange the pepper, courgette and onion on the base of the pan. Sprinkle over the parsley and season with salt and pepper. Cook over a medium heat for 3–4 minutes.

On a lightly floured surface, roll out the pastry. Cut out a circle slightly larger than the base of the pan. Put the pastry on top of the vegetables, trim off any excess pastry and press it down gently with your fingers. Bake in the oven for about 15–18 minutes, or until the pastry is golden brown.

Meanwhile, to make the relish, put the tomatoes, garlic, coriander and onion in a food processor and process until smooth. Season with salt and pepper.

To make the fritters, heat the sunflower oil in a deep frying-pan or wok. Put the eggs in a shallow bowl and season them and put the flour on a plate and season it. Dip the aubergine and courgette slices in the egg and then coat them in the flour. Deep-fry them a few at a time, until they are golden and crisp. Drain them on kitchen paper and keep them warm until you are ready to serve.

Remove the tart from the oven and invert it on to a plate. Serve the vegetable fritters with the tomato relish separately.

READY STEADY COOK Tips

Always deep-fry ingredients a few at a time so they are not crowded in the pan. If you put in too many at once, you will reduce the temperature of the oil and the food will not crisp.

The original tarte tatin is made with apples, but you can apply the same upside-down principle to all sorts of interesting fruits or vegetables.

Coat the aubergines and courgettes with egg and flour only when you are ready to put them straight into the hot oil, otherwise they will go soggy.

You can make your own pastry, if you prefer, but the ready-to-roll versions in the chill cabinet or freezer at the supermarket are excellent quality and save a lot of time.

L E S L E Y   W A T E R S

LAZY LASAGNE

Spinach and mushroom baked lasagne and open lasagne

Robin Ballance from London wanted a recipe for lasagne which, unlike his own, didn't taste like 'wallpaper paste'. Lesley obliged with not one but two lasagne ideas, using the classic combination for vegetarian lasagne of spinach and mushrooms.

SERVES 4	100 ml (3$^1/_2$ fl oz) white wine
225 g (8 oz) fresh spinach	25 g (1 oz) parmesan cheese, grated
350 g (12 oz) fresh or pre-cooked	100 g (4 oz) mozzarella cheese
lasagne sheets	
200 ml (7 fl oz) olive oil	**FOR THE OPEN LASAGNE**
$^1/_2$ onion, chopped	Small handful of fresh basil
250 g (9 oz) chestnut mushrooms, sliced	2 garlic cloves, peeled
Salt and freshly ground black pepper	1 tablespoon parmesan cheese, grated
	1 teaspoon ground turmeric
FOR THE BAKED LASAGNE	tablespoons chopped fresh flatleaf parsley
150 ml (5 fl oz) double cream	1 tablespoon lemon juice
1 tablespoon wholegrain French mustard	1 tomato, sliced, to garnish

Pre-heat the oven to gas mark 7, 220°C, 425°F. Put two-thirds of the spinach in a saucepan, season with a little salt and pepper and put on the lid. Let the spinach cook in its own juices, until wilted. Drain and keep warm.

Cook the pasta sheets in a large pan of salted, boiling water, according to the packet instructions. Drain the pasta and refresh it in cold water.

Heat 2 tablespoons of the oil in a frying-pan. Add the onion and cook until softened. Add the mushrooms and cook for 2–3 more minutes. Season, put half the mixture in a bowl and keep warm.

To make the baked lasagne, add the cream, mustard and wine to the frying-pan and cook for 2 minutes.

VEGETARIAN DISHES

Reserve half the lasagne sheets. Grease a small, shallow lasagne dish and put half of the remaining lasagne sheets to fit the base. Pour over half the sauce, scatter on a little parmesan and top with a layer of spinach. Repeat the layers of lasagne, mushroom, parmesan and spinach and then add the drained mozzarella cheese and remaining parmesan. Bake for 10–15 minutes, until golden brown.

To make the pesto for the open lasagne, put the basil and garlic in a food processor and chop them. Add 150 ml (5 fl oz) of the oil and the parmesan and process until the mixture is well blended and fairly finely chopped.

Heat the remaining oil in another frying-pan and add the turmeric and parsley. Halve the remaining pasta sheets and fry them for 1 minute, turning frequently until they are heated through.

To assemble the open lasagne, put a layer of fried pasta on a plate, pile on the reserved warm mushroom mixture and drizzle over half the pesto. Top with more pasta and pesto and garnish with slices of tomato. Serve the remaining spinach, shredded and flavoured with a little lemon juice and salt and pepper, separately.

READY STEADY COOK Tips

Pre-cooked lasagne sheets simply need to be rinsed in hot water before assembling the lasagne.

When warming the sauce in the pan, scrape up any oil and juices so that you retain all the flavour of the fried vegetables.

Freshly grated parmesan tastes better than the ready-grated tubs and, being a hard cheese, keeps fairly well. If you do have any left over, try grating it over steamed vegetables or sprinkling on soup.

LESLEY WATERS

READY, TEDDY, FETA

Filo roulade and feta toasties with salsa

If you go down to the woods today, you'll find Glaswegian teddy bear fanatic Chris Conran – a man fed up with meat dishes. He didn't come in disguise but he was certainly surprised by Lesley's delicious concoction of vegetables and feta cheese. He even brought his favourite teddy along for its own picnic!

SERVES 2–3

8 sheets of filo pastry
Olive oil

FOR THE FILLING

1 courgette, chopped
Juice of 1 lemon
185 g (6½ oz) tin of pitted black olives in brine, drained and chopped
200 g (7 oz) feta cheese
2 tomatoes, roughly chopped
½ red onion, roughly chopped
Handful of fresh basil leaves
Freshly ground black pepper

FOR THE TOASTIES

1 tablespoon olive oil
1 teaspoon ground turmeric
2 thick slices of country-style bread

FOR THE SALSA

2 tablespoons olive oil
1 courgette, sliced lengthways in thin strips
½ red onion, roughly chopped
2 garlic cloves, chopped
1 tablespoon chopped fresh parsley
2 tomatoes, roughly chopped
1 tablespoon balsamic vinegar
Pinch of sugar
Salt and freshly ground black pepper

Pre-heat the oven to gas mark 7, 220°C, 425°F. Put a clean tea towel on the work surface and lay six sheets of filo pastry on it, overlapping the sheets, to form a large rectangle. Brush the filo with olive oil.

In a bowl, mix together the courgette, lemon juice, half the olives, half the feta, crumbled, tomatoes and onion. Spread the mixture over the filo and scatter on most of the basil leaves, reserving a few of the best to garnish. Season with pepper. Using the tea towel, roll the filo

14

into a cylinder. Put it on a greased baking sheet, in a horseshoe shape. If there are any cracks, patch them with the remaining filo. Brush with a little oil and bake for 15 minutes, or until the pastry is golden brown.

Gently heat the oil and the turmeric in a small frying-pan. Cut out two discs of bread, using a 5 cm (2 in) cutter. Fry the bread for 1–2 minutes, turning frequently, until golden and crisp. Place on a baking sheet. Cut the remaining feta in half and put a piece on each disc. Bake for 5 minutes, or until the feta is soft and starting to brown.

For the salsa, put a tablespoon of olive oil in another frying-pan and fry the courgette and onion until golden. Add the garlic, parsley, tomatoes, balsamic vinegar, sugar, remaining olives and another tablespoon of olive oil. Season with salt and pepper, allow to warm through and remove from the heat.

To serve, put a toastie on each plate and top with salsa. Garnish with reserved basil leaves. Serve the filo roulade separately.

READY STEADY COOK Tips
Frozen filo pastry is a wonderful standby to keep in the freezer. Defrost thoroughly before using, and keep any sheets you are about to use covered with a damp cloth while you are preparing a dish so that they do not dry out and become too crumbly to manage.

Make sure the oil is hot enough before adding the bread otherwise it will soak up too much oil. It should start to sizzle as soon as it enters the pan.

These filling ingredients will also make a delicious fresh salad.

KEVIN WOODFORD

ANNIE'S ARTICHOKES WITH A BIT ON THE SIDE

Globe artichoke with two dressings and vegetable hors d'oeuvre with two dressings

Rock-jiving Anne Taylor simply wanted to jive up her artichokes! Kevin came up with this idea for artichokes with a mushroom and a cream dressing and also two dressings for a mixture of vegetable hors d'oeuvre.

SERVES 4
Juice of 1 lemon
4 globe artichokes
Salt and freshly ground black pepper

FOR THE MUSHROOM DRESSING
100 g (4 oz) butter
3 garlic cloves, finely chopped
1 white onion, finely chopped
12 open-cup mushrooms, finely chopped
3 tablespoons brandy
3 tablespoons chopped fresh coriander

FOR THE CREAM DRESSING
6 egg yolks
350 g (12 oz) unsalted butter, melted
3 tablespoons double cream

FOR THE VINAIGRETTE DRESSING
6 tablespoons good olive oil
2 tablespoons white-wine vinegar
2 teaspoons French mustard

FOR THE PAPRIKA AND CREAM DRESSING
100 ml (4 fl oz) double cream
1 teaspoon paprika
Lemon juice

FOR THE HORS D'OEUVRE
1 apple
Juice of 1 lemon
1 large celeriac, peeled and grated
4 beetroot, peeled and chopped
1 white onion, finely chopped
2 tablespoons chopped fresh parsley
2 tablespoons chopped fresh coriander
8 carrots, grated
1 large mooli, peeled and grated

Heat a saucepan of water and add half the lemon juice. Remove the outer leaves from the artichokes, trim the base and remove the prickles, to leave the heart. Scoop out the centre, leaving a hollow. Put the artichokes in the pan and leave to simmer for about 20–25 minutes, or until the outside leaves will pull out easily. Remove, drain and set aside.

Meanwhile, melt the butter in a small saucepan and add the garlic, the onion and most of the mushrooms. Season with salt and pepper and cook until softened. Add the brandy and set alight, tilting the pan until the flames die down. Cook for a further 3–4 minutes. Add the coriander and immediately remove from the heat and spoon into the centre of the artichokes. Put on heatproof plates.

Pre-heat the grill to hot. Put the egg yolks in a glass bowl over a pan of simmering water (which should not touch the bottom of the bowl). Gradually add the butter and whisk continuously. Add the cream, pour over the artichokes and place under the grill for 4–5 minutes.

Mix together the ingredients for the vinaigrette dressing and season to taste. Do the same for the paprika and cream dressing, adding a good squeeze of lemon juice, to taste, with the salt and pepper.

Slice the apple and squeeze some of the lemon juice over the apple slices. Combine the celeriac and beetroot and toss in some of the vinaigrette dressing.

Add the onion, with the parsley and coriander, to the carrots. Toss in the remaining vinaigrette.

Add the reserved mushrooms to the mooli and toss in the cream and paprika dressing.

To serve, put each artichoke in the centre of a plate and alternate the apple, celeriac, carrot and mooli hors d'oeuvre around the edge.

KEVIN WOODFORD

DAWN'S DELIGHTFUL TIMBALES

Courgette timbales with tomato sauce and potato nests

Never having done anything with a vegetable apart from boil it, Dawn Adams thought it was about tiime she learnt to do more. These timbales are easy to do and thoroughly live up to their name.

SERVES 2

FOR THE TIMBALES
1 medium-sized courgette and
1 small courgette
1 tablespoon olive oil
50 g (2 oz) mushrooms, roughly chopped
150 g (5 oz) tomatoes, skinned, seeded and chopped
1 garlic clove, crushed
4 tablespoons white wine
50 g (2 oz) fresh breadcrumbs
$^1/_2$ teaspoon tomato purée
Salt and freshly ground black pepper
Sprigs of flatleaf parsley, to garnish

FOR THE POTATO NESTS
1 large baking potato
2 tablespoons double cream or milk
50 g (2 oz) Cheshire cheese, grated
Salt and freshly ground black pepper

FOR THE SAUCE
1 tablespoon olive oil
4 spring onions, finely sliced
75 g (3 oz) mushrooms, roughly chopped
150 g (5 oz) tomatoes, skinned, seeded and chopped
75 ml ($2^3/_4$ fl oz) white wine
$^1/_2$ teaspoon tomato purée
Salt and freshly ground black pepper

Using a potato peeler, cut six thin, lengthways slices of courgette and blanch them in boiling water for 30 seconds. Refresh under cold water and set aside.

Chop the remaining courgettes. Heat the oil in a pan, add the courgettes, mushrooms, tomatoes and garlic and cook for a minute.

VEGETARIAN DISHES

Add the wine, breadcrumbs and tomato purée and season with salt and pepper. Cook for 8–10 minutes.

Meanwhile, prick the potato skin with a sharp knife and microwave it on full power for 6–8 minutes, or until tender.

Line two timbale moulds or 10 cm (4 in) ramekin dishes with cling film. Line the moulds with courgette slices, leaving the ends of the slices to overhang the edges of the moulds. Fill with the courgette and mushroom mixture and bring the ends of the courgette slices back, to cover the filling. Cover with cling film to enclose courgettes and filling. Stand the moulds in a pan of barely simmering water (the water should come only halfway up the sides of the moulds) and poach for 5 minutes making sure the water does not bubble over the tops of the moulds.

To make the sauce, heat the oil in another pan, add the spring onions, mushrooms and tomatoes and cook for 3 minutes. Add the wine and tomato purée and season with salt and pepper. Cook for 4–5 minutes, stirring occasionally.

Pre-heat the grill to hot. Cut the potato in half and scoop out the flesh. Mash with the cream and season well. Pipe or spoon two 10 cm (4 in) nests on to flameproof serving plates. Alternatively, pipe or spoon the potato back into the skins. Sprinkle the cheese in the middle and grill for 2 minutes, until golden.

To serve, turn the timbales out on to serving plates and spoon the sauce around them. Garnish with flatleaf parsley and serve with the potato nests.

READY STEADY COOK Tips
Blanching the courgette slices makes them tender and flexible for lining the ramekins.

Microwave 'baked' potatoes are a wonderful standby for a quick and filling lunch. Top them with grated cheese and herbs, mix in some flaked tuna and mayonnaise, top with a spoonful of bolognaise sauce or stir in a little pesto.

KEVIN WOODFORD

ANGIE'S SUPER SUPPER SURPRISE

Semolina gnocchi with spicy tomato sauce

Single mum Angie Tindall wondered if the thing she hated most in the world –
semolina – could actually be turned into something delicious. These delightful gnocchi –
Italian-style dumplings – convinced her.

SERVES 2	FOR THE SAUCE
FOR THE GNOCCHI	15 g ($^1/_2$ oz) butter
450 ml (15 fl oz) milk	$^1/_2$ onion, finely chopped
75 g (3 oz) semolina	$^1/_2$ red pepper, seeded and sliced
$^1/_2$ teaspoon grated nutmeg	$^1/_2$ leek, sliced
1 egg yolk	1 garlic clove, crushed
25 g (1 oz) butter	1 tablespoon chopped fresh coriander
1 tablespoon double cream	1 tablespoon chopped fresh parsley
75 g (3 oz) parmesan cheese, grated	400 g (14 oz) tin of chopped tomatoes
Salt and freshly ground black pepper	Tabasco sauce
	4 tablespoons tomato purée
	Salt and freshly ground black pepper

To make the gnocchi, bring the milk to the boil and stir in the
semolina, keeping the pan on the heat. The mixture will begin to
thicken. Add the nutmeg and egg yolk, stirring continuously. Season
with salt and pepper. Add the butter, cream and half the parmesan
and mix thoroughly. Spoon the semolina into a small, shallow,
buttered ovenproof dish and leave to cool while you make the sauce.

To make the sauce, melt the butter in a saucepan and sauté the
onion, pepper, leek, garlic and herbs for 5 minutes. Add the
tomatoes, 4–5 drops of Tabasco sauce and tomato purée and leave
to simmer for 10 minutes, stirring occasionally. Add salt and pepper to
season if required.

Pre-heat the grill to hot. Turn the semolina out and cut out circles from it, with a pastry cutter. Replace the rounds in the dish, sprinkle over the remaining parmesan and grill for 4–5 minutes until the cheese melts and turns golden brown.

To serve, place the gnocchi on a plate and surround with the sauce.

K E V I N   W O O D F O R D

MEXICAN ROSINA

Spicy-bean tortillas with cheese and avocado cream

Gary, from Telford, told Kevin that he'd like something Mexican and something plentiful enough to satisfy his young daughter's appetite – 'She's a small lass but I've seen her devour a whole trout!'.

SERVES 4
6 large soft tortillas
Salt and freshly ground black pepper

FOR THE FILLING
2 tablespoons olive oil
1 garlic clove, crushed
1 small onion, finely chopped
400 g (14 oz) tin of chopped tomatoes
400 g (14 oz) tin of kidney beans, drained and rinsed
2 teaspoons Worcestershire sauce
1 tablespoon tomato purée
1 teaspoon chilli powder

5 tablespoons white wine
3–4 fresh basil leaves, chopped

FOR THE CHEESE SAUCE
40 g (1½ oz) butter
40 g (1½ oz) plain flour
600 ml (1 pint) milk
75 g (3 oz) mild Cheddar cheese, grated
Salt and freshly ground black pepper

FOR THE AVOCADO CREAM
1 avocado, peeled and stoned
150 ml (5 fl oz) double cream
Juice of ½ lemon

Pre-heat the oven to gas mark 6, 200°C, 400°F. To make the filling, heat the oil in a saucepan and add the garlic, onion, tomatoes, kidney beans, Worcestershire sauce, tomato purée, chilli powder, wine and basil. Cook for 8–10 minutes.

21

To make the cheese sauce, melt the butter in a small pan and add the flour. Mix together for a minute or two and then gradually add the milk and stir until thickened and just bubbling. Off the heat, add the cheese, season and whisk until smooth.

Line a buttered, shallow, ovenproof dish with four tortillas. Make sure these are slightly overlapping the edge of the dish. Pour on the bean filling and then cover with remaining tortillas. Pour on the cheese sauce. Bake for 15 minutes.

For the dip, blend the avocado, cream, lemon juice and seasoning, using a fork or in a food processor. Serve as an accompaniment to the tortillas.

READY STEADY COOK Tip
Serve the avocado dip on its own, as a starter, with corn chips and/or crudités to dip in.

LESLEY WATERS

THE ITALIAN CONNECTION

Tuna pizzas with rustic bread and olive and mushroom salad

A designer of bank notes, Lionel Walker from Amersham failed to bring us any samples. Instead he wanted Lesley to show him the techniques of Italian cooking. Lesley obliged with these tuna pizzas and rustic-style bread and Lionel said the end result looked like 'an artist's palette'.

SERVES 2
280 g (about 10 oz) packet of bread mix
40 g (1½ oz) sun-dried tomatoes in oil
10-11 tablespoons warm water
2 tomatoes, skinned, seeded and chopped
185 g (about 7 oz) tin of tuna in brine, drained
4 tablespoons grated mozzarella cheese
2 tablespoons chopped fresh basil

FOR THE SALAD   juice of ¹/₂ lemon
2 eggs   1 tablespoon snipped fresh chives
5 tablespoons good olive oil   ¹/₂ cos lettuce
100 g (4 oz) button mushrooms   6 pitted green olives
2 garlic cloves, crushed   Salt and freshly ground black pepper

Pre-heat the oven to gas mark 7, 220°C, 425°F. Put the bread mix in a food processor or mixing bowl, together with 2 tablespoons of oil from the sun-dried tomatoes and some water. Process or mix by hand, to form a soft dough. Knead for 3–4 minutes on a floured surface.

Halve the dough and roll out one half. Chop four of the sun-dried tomatoes and sprinkle them over the dough. Fold over the dough and re-roll it, to make a 23 cm (9 in) round. Score halfway through the dough, to expose the tomatoes, brush with a little more of their oil. Shape into a compact oval shape and put on a greased baking sheet.

Divide the remaining dough into two and roll out each piece, to make 18 cm (7 in) individual pizzas. Transfer the pizza bases to a greased baking sheet and spread a tablespoon of the chopped tomatoes over each. Sprinkle over a little of the tuna, 2 tablespoons of the cheese and any remaining sun-dried tomatoes on to each pizza.

Bake both trays of dough in the oven for 10 minutes, until brown and crisp. Sprinkle the chopped basil over the pizzas just before the end of cooking time. Brush the tomato bread with a tablespoon of the oil from the sun-dried tomatoes.

Meanwhile, hard-boil the eggs for 6–8 minutes, drain them and put them in cold, running water, to cool. Shell the eggs and quarter them.

Heat 2 tablespoons of the olive oil, add the mushrooms and garlic and sauté over medium heat, for 3–4 minutes.

To make the dressing, pour the remaining 3 tablespoons of olive oil into a bowl or jar, add the lemon juice, chives and salt and pepper to taste. Mix thoroughly. Pour over the mushrooms, to warm the dressing.

Tear the lettuce leaves into pieces and put them on a serving plate or in a bowl. Spoon over the remaining tuna and the egg quarters and olives and pour over the mushrooms and dressing just before serving. Serve the pizzas with the salad, and the rustic bread on a board.

FISH AND SHELLFISH

GET YOUR SKATES ON - 25

CRACKINGLY CRISP CONTAINERS
WITH COD STEAKS - 27

OUR PLAICE - 28

TEN TORS TUNA - 30

DANIELLA'S DELIGHTFUL DEEP-SEA PASTA - 31

AROMATIC FEAST - 32

BENNETT'S BASIL BISQUE AND
DRIGHLINGTON DELIGHT - 34

LORNA'S LUSCIOUS LOBSTER - 36

GLENN'S PAISLEY SURPRISE - 38

ANDREW'S FISH PIE - 40

SARAH'S MEDLEY OF FRESH FISH ON A BED OF
CHABLIS AND SPRING ONION SAUCE - 42

FISH AND SHELLFISH

LESLEY WATERS

GET YOUR SKATES ON

Skate wing with black-butter sauce with capers, and fennel and potato rösti and warm salad

The office was flooded with fan mail after Norman Ellis came on the show and told Fern he was looking for a wife! He will be able to charm the lucky lady with this excellent fish recipe that's just right for two.

SERVES 2

FOR THE SKATE
100 ml (3$^1/_2$ fl oz) white wine
3 thyme sprigs
1 bay leaf
6 black peppercorns
Slice of lemon
1 tablespoon white-wine vinegar
2 skate wings

FOR THE RÖSTIS
1 large potato, peeled and coarsely grated
2 tablespoons olive oil
1 fennel bulb, quartered and sliced thinly
6 black peppercorns
Dried oregano
Freshly ground black pepper

FOR THE WARM SALAD
500 g (1 lb 2 oz) broccoli, cut in florets
1 tablespoon olive oil
1 yellow pepper, seeded and chopped
Small handful of basil leaves
Salt and freshly ground black pepper

FOR THE DRESSING
75 ml (2 $^3/_4$ fl oz) white wine
1 tablespoon olive oil
1 teaspoon Dijon mustard
1 tablespoon white-wine vinegar

FOR THE SAUCE
50 g (2 oz) unsalted butter
2 tablespoons caper
Lemon juice

Bring a saucepan and a shallow pan of water to the boil. Dry the grated potato in a tea towel.

Put the wine, thyme, bay leaf, black peppercorns, lemon slice and vinegar in the shallow pan with the water and bring back to a simmer for 4 minutes.

Meanwhile, make the röstis. Heat a tablespoon of the oil and gently fry the fennel and black peppercorns for about 8 minutes. In a bowl, mix together the fennel and potato. Add a good pinch of oregano and season with pepper. Set aside until cool enough to handle, then mould into two r[something] rästis (flat, pattie shapes). Heat the remaining oil in a small frying-pan and fry one rösti for 2–3 minutes, until golden brown underneath. Turn it by putting a baking tray on top and inverting the frying-pan. Repeat to brown the other side and then keep warm while you fry the second in the same way. While the rästis are frying add the fish to the shallow pan and poach gently for 10–12 minutes, turning once until firm and opaque. Keep the rästis warm while you make the salad.

For the salad, put the broccoli into the saucepan of boiling water and cook for about 3 minutes. Drain and refresh in cold water. Heat the oil in a wok and stir-fry the pepper and broccoli for 2–3 minutes until tender but still firm. Season. Mix together all the ingredients for the dressing, pour into the wok and add some basil leaves.

Melt the butter in a small frying-pan and cook the capers, with a squeeze of lemon juice, until the butter is dark. This takes about 4 minutes over high heat.

To serve, put the rästis and skate wings on two warmed plates and pour the caper sauce over the fish. Serve with the broccoli and pepper salad.

READY STEADY COOK Tips

Try making rösti with sliced onion and bacon to serve with continental sausages or grilled meats.

Frying the spices imparts a wonderful flavour to the frying oil.

Experiment with other spices for different flavour effects.
Like any fish, skate should be very fresh. It has a slight ammonia smell when it is past its best.

L E S L E Y   W A T E R S

CRACKINGLY CRISP CONTAINERS WITH COD STEAKS

Cod steaks with aromatic stewed peppers, tomato and cheese filo parcels and roasted-tomato salad

On a programme broadcast near to Christmas, Huw Dennis said he was already fed up with the idea of turkey and spuds, so he presented Lesley with fish and pastry and asked her to come up with an original idea.

SERVES 2

FOR THE PEPPERS
2 tablespoons olive oil
$1/_2$ green pepper, seeded and sliced
$1/_2$ yellow pepper, seeded and sliced
1 garlic clove, crushed
1 tablespoon chopped fresh mixed herbs
$1/_2$ lemon
Salt and freshly ground black pepper

1 tablespoon chopped fresh sage
4 filo pastry sheets
Salt and freshly ground black pepper

FOR THE SALAD
4 tomatoes, halved with cores removed
2 tablespoons olive oil
2 tablespoons chopped fresh basil
Salt and freshly ground black pepper

FOR THE FILO PARCELS
3 tablespoons olive oil
1 small onion, chopped
4 tomatoes, cut in wedges
50 g (2 oz) Cheddar cheese, grated

FOR THE COD
1 tablespoon olive oil
2 x 150 g (5 oz) cod steaks
4 tablespoons white wine
Salt and freshly ground black pepper

Pre-heat the oven to gas mark 6, 200°C, 400°F. To make the peppers, heat the oil in a pan, add the peppers, garlic and herbs and season with salt and pepper. Squeeze in the lemon juice and add the squeezed lemon half. Cover and cook gently for 15 minutes, stirring now and again.

Meanwhile, make the filo parcels. Heat a tablespoon of oil in another pan, add the onion and cook for 3 minutes. Add the tomatoes and cook for 2 minutes. Off the heat, stir in the cheese, sage and seasoning.

Cut each sheet of filo pastry in half to give two squares. Brush one square of filo pastry with a little oil and place another square on top. Spoon a quarter of the tomato and cheese mixture into the centre. Lift the corners of the filo over the filling and pinch the edges together, to seal and form a parcel. Put on a greased baking sheet and brush with 1 tablespoon of oil. Repeat with the remaining filo and filling, to make four parcels. Bake for 6–8 minutes, until golden brown.

To make the salad, put the tomato halves on a baking sheet. Drizzle the oil over them, scatter the chopped basil over the top and season well. Roast for 12–15 minutes, until the skins are lightly charred.

For the cod, heat the oil in a frying-pan, add the steaks, wine and seasoning and cook for 8 minutes, turning once.

To serve, spoon the peppers over the cod steaks (discarding the lemon half) and serve with the filo parcels. Serve on a plate with the roasted tomato salad, garnished with basil leaves.

LESLEY WATERS

OUR PLAICE

Pan-fried plaice fillets and tartare sauce, with grilled courgettes, potatoes and petits pois

Philip Singh wanted to be treated to a fish dish because his wife, Corrine, hates fish and so he has to go without it at home.

SERVES 2
FOR THE COURGETTES
2 courgettes, sliced lengthways
1 tablespoon olive oil
juice of 1/2 lemon

Salt and freshly ground black pepper

FOR THE POTATOES
225 g (8 oz) potatoes, cut in
2 cm (3/4 in) chunks

28

FISH AND SHELLFISH

100 g (4 oz) petits pois or peas

3 tablespoons olive oil

15 g (½ oz) sun-dried tomatoes, chopped

2 tablespoons chopped fresh dill

Salt and freshly ground black pepper

FOR THE PLAICE

3 shallots, quartered

1 medium-size plaice, cut in 4 fillets and skinned

Plain flour

25 g (1 oz) unsalted butter

Salt and freshly ground black pepper

FOR THE SAUCE

100 g (4 oz) Greek yoghurt

1 tablespoon gherkins, chopped

1 tablespoon capers, chopped

Salt and freshly ground black pepper

TO GARNISH

Chopped fresh parsley

Orange wedges

Pre-heat the grill to hot. Mix the oil and the lemon juice in a small bowl and season with salt and pepper. Dip the courgette slices in the marinade to coat. Then place them on the grill rack and grill for 12–15 minutes, turning once, until well browned, brushing with marinade halfway through cooking.

Meanwhile, cook the potatoes in boiling water for 8–10 minutes, or until tender.

Now begin cooking the plaice. Melt the butter in a large frying-pan and cook the shallots for 3 minutes, stirring occasionally.

Lightly dust the fillets with flour and season well. Add the fillets to the pan and fry for 3–4 minutes, turning once, until golden.

Cook the petits pois for 3 minutes. Drain the potatoes and peas and put in a serving bowl. Add the oil, sun-dried tomatoes, dill and seasoning and toss until well mixed.

Mix the Greek yoghurt, gherkins, capers and seasoning, to make a tartare sauce. Spoon into a serving bowl.

To serve, put the fillets on warmed serving plates, scatter the shallots over the top and arrange the courgettes to one side. Sprinkle the parsley over the fish and shallots and garnish with orange wedges. Serve the potatoes and peas and the tartare sauce separately.

L E S L E Y   W A T E R S

TEN TORS TUNA

Griddled tuna steak, with roasted tomatoes, cardamom beans and cheese-and-mustard potatoes

Busy training youngsters for The Ten Tors, Pat Read, from Exeter, needed something quick, easy and healthy. She brought along some Curworthy cheese, a local Okehampton favourite, with a unique flavour but mature Cheddar works just as well.

SERVES 2–3

FOR THE POTATOES
25 g (1 oz) butter
$1/_2$ onion, finely chopped
900 g (2 lb) new potatoes, washed and thickly sliced
2 bay leaves
150 ml (5 fl oz) white wine
450 ml (15 fl oz) vegetable stock
150 g (5 oz) mature Cheddar cheese, grated
1 tablespoon Dijon mustard
Salt and freshly ground black pepper

FOR THE TOMATOES
5 large plum tomatoes
$1/_2$ onion, sliced
$1/_2$ teaspoon chopped fresh thyme leaves
2 tablespoons olive oil
1 teaspoon Worcestershire sauce

FOR THE TUNA
2 tablespoons olive oil
1 tablespoon soy sauce
350 g (12 oz) tuna steak
Salt and freshly ground black pepper

FOR THE BEANS
150 g (5 oz) green beans
5 green cardamom pods
1 tablespoon olive oil

Pre-heat the oven to gas mark 6, 200°C, 400°F. Melt the butter in a large pan and add the onion and potatoes. Add the bay leaves, season with salt and pepper and sauté for 2 minutes. Add the wine and stock, cover and leave to simmer until the potatoes are tender, about 10–15 minutes. Make sure the pan does not dry out.

Meanwhile, put the tomatoes and sliced onion in a bowl and add the thyme, oil and Worcestershire sauce. Stir well, place on a baking sheet and roast for 12 minutes, until skins are lightly charred.

FISH AND SHELLFISH

Mix the oil, soy sauce and seasoning and coat the tuna steak in the mixture. Heat a griddle pan or large, heavy-based frying-pan over very high heat. Griddle the tuna for 2–3 minutes on each side, until seared and cooked through. Cut the tuna into four steaks.

Meanwhile, blanch the beans in boiling water for 3 minutes. Drain and refresh under cold water. Cut in half. Crush the cardamom pods and extract the seeds. Heat the oil in a sauté pan and add the beans and the cardamom seeds. Allow to warm through.

Add the cheese and mustard to the potatoes and remaining stock. Stir to coat the potatoes and leave them in the covered pan until the cheese has melted.To serve, spoon the potatoes on a plate, top with the tuna steak and pile the tomatoes and beans around.

KEVIN WOODFORD

DANIELLA'S DELIGHTFUL DEEP-SEA PASTA

Pasta spirals in creamy seafood and tomato sauce, with grilled mussels and herby breadcrumbs

Before getting married, Kelly Gatta had never cooked, so she needed some help, particularly with seafood, which does need careful handling.

SERVES 2
175 g (6 oz) pasta twists
FOR THE SAUCE
2 tablespoons olive oil
8 raw tiger prawns, heads removed, shelled, shells reserved and bodies cut in 1 cm (1/2 in) chunks
10 cooked green-lipped New Zealand mussels, 4 shelled and chopped
10 medium tomatoes, quartered
150 ml (5 fl oz) red wine

2 tablespoons chopped fresh coriander
5 squid, cleaned and cut in rings
2 tablespoons double cream

FOR THE HERBY BREADCRUMBS
1/4 small baguette
2 tablespoons chopped fresh basil
2 tablespoons chopped fresh parsley
2 tablespoons snipped fresh chives
1 garlic clove, crushed
2 tablespoons olive oil

31

Cook the pasta in salted, boiling water, according to the packet instructions. When cooked, drain and keep warm, tossed in a little oil, if necessary.

Meanwhile, to make the sauce, first heat a tablespoon of oil in a small pan and cook the prawn shells, four mussel shells, tomatoes, wine and coriander for 5 minutes. Remove the prawn and mussel shells and leave the sauce to simmer for a further 10 minutes. Liquidize the sauce and then pass it through a sieve.

Sauté the squid rings and prawns in the remaining oil for 2 minutes. Add the shelled mussels and the drained pasta and cook for a further minute. Add the tomato sauce and cream and mix thoroughly.

To make the grilled mussels, pre-heat the grill to hot. Put the bread, basil, parsley, chives and garlic in a food processor and process to fine crumbs. Slowly pour in the oil and mix well. Spread the herby breadcrumbs on the mussels in their shells and grill for 3–4 minutes, or until lightly golden brown.

Divide the pasta and sauce between two warmed serving dishes and garnish with the grilled mussels.

LESLEY WATERS

AROMATIC FEAST

Creamy fish curry with savoury rice and spicy green beans

Single and in search of a date, John Llewellyn asked Lesley for some culinary tips to impress the ladies. We are sure that no one could resist this wonderful and healthy fish curry.

SERVES 2	450 ml (³/₄ pint) water
FOR THE RICE	2–3 bay leaves
1 tablespoon olive oil	1 lime, very finely chopped, including the skin
1 onion, chopped	Salt and freshly ground black pepper
150 g (5 oz) basmati rice, washed	

Above: The Italian Connection (page 22).

Above: Daniella's Delightful Deep-Sea Pasta (page 31).
Below: Goulash and Mash (page 66).

FOR THE CURRY
2 tablespoons sunflower oil
1 onion, chopped
2 green chillies, seeded if wished
and finely chopped
2 tablespoons finely chopped
fresh root ginger
1 teaspoon ground turmeric
1 tablespoon garam masala
1 teaspoon curry powder
150 ml (5 fl oz) white wine

150 ml (5 fl oz) water or vegetable stock
2 coley fillets, skinned and cut in
2.5 cm (1 in) pieces
4 tablespoons curd cheese
2 tablespoons hot water

FOR THE BEANS
150 g (5 oz) green beans
1 tablespoon sunflower oil
$^1/_2$ tablespoon garam masala
Coriander leaves, to garnish (optional)

To make the rice, heat the oil in a high-sided pan and sauté the onion for 4 minutes, or until it is translucent and soft. Add the rice and stir to coat it completely in oil. Pour in enough water to cover the rice, add the bay leaves and bring to the boil. Leave the rice covered to simmer until it has absorbed all the water. Stir in the lime just before serving. Season to taste.

For the fish curry, heat the oil and fry the onion until soft. Add the chillies and continue to cook for a minute. Then add the ginger, turmeric, garam masala and curry powder. Stir to make sure all the spices are coated in the oil. Pour in the wine and water or stock, bring to the boil and leave to simmer for 5 minutes, stirring occasionally.

Add the coley to the sauce and cook gently until the fish becomes firm and turns white, about 4–5 minutes.

Mix together the curd cheese and water. Stir the cheese into the fish curry and cook over a medium heat for a minute. Add extra water or stock if the sauce becomes too thick.

For the spicy beans, cook the beans in salted, boiling water for 5 minutes. Drain the beans. Heat the oil in a sauté or small frying-pan, add the beans and garam masala and cook for 2–3 minutes.

To serve, spoon the rice on to a large platter. Arrange the fish curry around the rice and garnish with fresh coriander leaves, if you like. Serve the beans separately.

BENNETT'S BASIL BISQUE AND DRIGHLINGTON DELIGHT

Simple paella, and basil and prawn bisque with garlic croûtons

Val Bennett had a dilemma: what on earth was she going to do with the neglected jar of artichokes in her cupboard? *Ready Steady Cook* and Kevin came up with the perfect answer.

SERVES 4

FOR THE PAELLA
2 tablespoons extra-virgin olive oil
350 g (12 oz) long-grain rice
1 slice of onion
Bunch of spring onions, chopped, green tops reserved
Small piece of fresh red chilli, seeded and chopped
1 red pepper, seeded and chopped
$1/2$ courgette, chopped
1 teaspoon ground turmeric
1 skinless, boneless chicken thigh, cut into 4 cm ($1^1/2$ in) cubes
1 garlic clove, crushed
350 g (12 oz) frozen peas
1 jar seasoned artichoke hearts, drained or 1 can artichoke hearts, drained
600 ml (1 pint) water
200 g (7 oz) cooked peeled prawns
150 g (5 oz) cooked shell-on prawns, heads removed and reserved
Salt and freshly ground black pepper

FOR THE BISQUE
2 tablespoons olive oil
1 tablespoon chopped fresh basil
1 tablespoon snipped fresh chives
1 slice of onion
1 garlic clove, crushed
75 g (3 oz) long-grain rice
2 tablespoons tomato purée
1.5 litres ($2^1/2$ pints) vegetable stock
300 ml (10 fl oz) white wine
Salt and freshly ground black pepper

FOR THE CROÛTONS
25 g (1 oz) butter
1 garlic clove, crushed
2 slices of bread, cubed

34

To make the paella, heat the oil in a deep saucepan. Add the rice, onion slice, the white of spring onion, chilli, pepper and courgette. Stir in the turmeric, chicken and garlic. Mix together and add the peas and artichokes. Pour in the water, stir well and bring just back to the boil. Season with salt and pepper. Leave to cook on a fairly low heat, until the rice has absorbed all the liquid. To check that the chicken is cooked, pierce with a skewer or sharp knife. If the juices run clear, the chicken is cooked.

To make the bisque, heat the oil in a saucepan. Put in the reserved prawn heads and green of spring onion, and the basil, chives, onion slice, garlic, rice, half the tomato purée, water and wine. Season and leave to reduce over a gentle heat for 15–20 minutes.

For the croûtons, melt the butter and add the garlic and bread cubes. Toss for 1–2 minutes until golden, drain on kitchen paper and keep warm.

Remove the prawn heads from the bisque, liquidize and pass it through a sieve. Return to the pan and add the remaining tomato purée. Heat through and season.

Stir the peeled prawns into the paella and cook for 2–3 minutes, to warm them through. Spoon the paella into a warmed serving dish and garnish it with the prawn tails. Pour the bisque into warmed soup bowls and garnish with the croûtons. Serve immediately.

READY STEADY COOK Tips
Cooked prawns only need to be warmed through in the paella. If you want to use uncooked prawns, cook them for a few minutes – just until they turn pink.

Paella can be made with a wide variety of ingredients, so if you have anything missing from your list or want to try making it with a different set of ingredients, there's no rules as long as it tastes good.

KEVIN WOODFORD

LORNA'S LUSCIOUS LOBSTER

Lobster in wine and cream sauce, with herby savoury rice

Lorna adored lobster but could never justify cooking it for herself until she was given one by a friendly local fisherman. Kevin added a delicious herby rice and a luxurious sauce for a fitting accompaniment to our most luxurious seafood.

SERVES 2	FOR THE LOBSTER
FOR THE RICE	1 medium cooked lobster
1 tablespoon olive oil	25 g (1 oz) butter
2 shallots, finely chopped	1 garlic clove, crushed
100 g (4 oz) long-grain rice	85 ml (3 fl oz) white wine
2 tablespoons chopped fresh dill	2 teaspoons Dijon mustard
1 tablespoon chopped fresh coriander	3 tablespoons double cream
1 tablespoon chopped fresh basil	Lemon juice
1 vegetable stock cube, dissolved in	1 egg yolk
850 ml (1½ pints) water	Lemon wedges, to garnish

To make the savoury rice, heat the oil in a heavy pan or frying-pan and fry a tablespoon of shallot for a minute. Add the rice and stir to coat it in oil. Mix the herbs together and add 2 tablespoons of herbs to the pan; stir and cook for another minute. Pour in the stock, bring to the boil and then leave to simmer on a low heat for 12–15 minutes, or until the rice has absorbed all the stock. Spoon the cooked rice into a large buttered ramekin dish.

Meanwhile, lay the lobster on its back and cut it in half from head to tail. Discard the stomach sac and intestinal tract. Scoop out all the white tail meat from both halves of the body, including the green meat. Wash and dry the shells. Cut off the legs and claws and remove as much meat as possible from them.

FISH AND SHELLFISH

Melt the butter in a small, heavy pan and sauté the garlic and the rest of the shallots and herbs. Pour in the wine and bring to the boil. Add the mustard and cream and leave to simmer for 3 minutes. Add the lobster meat and a squeeze of lemon juice. Cook for another minute to heat the meat through, then stir in the egg yolk. Be careful not to let the sauce boil at this point, or it will curdle.

To serve, spoon the lobster flesh and sauce back into the half shells. Turn out the rice on to a warmed serving dish, in a neat mound. Garnish with lemon wedges.

READY STEADY COOK Tips

Lobster is delicious but, for a cheaper alternative, buy a cooked, dressed crab and take all the meat out of the shell. Add to the sauce as for the lobster and serve piled back into the shell, with the savoury rice.

Crack the lobster claws firmly with the back of a knife to lift out the meat.

Shallots have a more delicate flavour than onions. They should be gently softened in the pan and not allowed to brown.

Any left-over rice can be served cold as a salad.

KEVIN WOODFORD

GLENN'S PAISLEY SURPRISE

Haddock mousses with white wine and cream sauce and baby vegetables

Having recently given birth to Glenn, Lorraine Corrigan, from Paisley, was keen to find an infallible recipe that she could whip up at any hour! The sauce for the dish is a variation of the classic French *beurre blanc*.

SERVES 2

FOR THE MOUSSES
225 g (8 oz) haddock fillet, skinned
1 egg white
2 tablespoons double cream
$^1/_2$ tablespoon snipped fresh chives
Handful of spinach leaves
Grated zest of $^1/_2$ lemon
Grated zest of $^1/_2$ lime
Salt and freshly ground black pepper

FOR THE SAUCE
150 ml (5 fl oz) white wine
2 tablespoons double cream
2 tablespoons snipped fresh chives
50 g (2 oz) unsalted butter, chopped

TO SERVE
2 carrots cut *à la Parisienne*
(see tip)
5 French beans, sliced diagonally
1 tablespoon olive oil
5 baby onions or shallots
85 ml (3 fl oz) chicken stock

Put the fish in a food processor and add the egg white. Process for a minute. Add 2 tablespoons of cream, a little at a time to ensure that it doesn't curdle. Add the chives and season with salt and pepper.

Soften the spinach leaves in boiling water for 2 minutes. Drain under cold running water.

Butter two ramekin dishes and line them with cling film. Line the dishes with the spinach leaves. Divide the lemon and lime zest between each. Spoon in the fish-mousse mixture. Half-fill a roasting tin with boiling water and put the ramekins in it, making sure the water comes no more than halfway up the sides of the dishes. Cook the mousses at a simmer for 15–20 minutes, or until the mousse mixture is firm to the touch and heated through.

To make the sauce, first reduce the wine by half. This takes 4–5 minutes over a high heat. Add 2 tablespoons of cream and the chives. Whisk in the butter, piece by piece, and cook for a further 2 minutes until the sauce is thick and creamy.

Cook the carrots in salted, boiling water for 4–5 minutes, add the beans and cook for a further 2–3 minutes until al dente (tender but still with a slight bite in the middle).

Heat the oil in a small frying-pan and sauté the baby onions for 2 minutes until lightly coloured. Add the chicken stock, cover and cook for 5 minutes until the onions are soft and translucent. Drain the onions and mix them with the carrots and beans.

To serve, turn out each mousse on to a serving plate. Arrange the vegetables on one side and surround everything with the sauce.

READY STEADY COOK Tips

To make carrots à la Parisienne, cut the carrots into squarish chunks and use a swivel vegetable peeler to shave off the corners to make little balls. Alternatively, cut peeled carrots into 4 cm (1¹/₂ in) chunks, then use a melon baller to scoop out balls of carrot.

Use small, tender spinach leaves if you can. If they have a thickish stem, hold the stem in your right hand and fold the leaf in half, with the veins outwards, with your left. Gently pull the stem upwards and it will pull away from the leaf.

Boiling a liquid to reduce it concentrates the flavours.

KEVIN WOODFORD

ANDREW'S FISH PIE

Cod in a creamy sauce, baked in filo pastry and served with mushroom sauce

With a strange addiction to fish-finger sandwiches (something that even his son Andrew finds disgusting), Dave Whittingham decided it was time to get 'posh with fish'.

SERVES 2

FOR THE PIE
75 g (3 oz) butter
50 g (2 oz) plain flour
300 ml (10 fl oz) milk
300 g (11 oz) cod fillet, skinned and cut in 1 cm ($1/2$ in) cubes
1 tablespoon olive oil
2 carrots, finely chopped
1 leek, thinly sliced
1 lemon grass stalk, thinly sliced
1 fresh red chilli, seeded and finely chopped
1 tablespoon chopped fresh dill
1 tablespoon chopped fresh flatleaf parsley
2 tablespoons chopped fresh basil
1 tablespoon white wine
Juice of $1/2$ lemon
Salt and freshly ground black pepper
4 filo pastry sheets

FOR THE MUSHROOM SAUCE
25 g (1 oz) butter
1 tablespoon white wine
100 g (4 oz) mushrooms, sliced
2 tablespoons double cream
Salt and freshly ground black pepper

Pre-heat the oven to gas mark 6, 200°C, 400°F. Melt the butter in a small pan and keep it warm.

To make the white sauce, put 5 tablespoons of the melted butter in another saucepan, add the flour, stir well and cook for 30 seconds. Slowly add the milk, stirring continuously, and bring to the boil. Off the heat, add a cube of cod and leave for the flavour to infuse.

Heat the oil and sauté the carrots, leek, lemon grass, chilli and herbs, until the carrots are soft. Stir in the wine and then add the white sauce and lemon juice and season with salt and black pepper.

40

Brush the filo pastry sheets with some of the remaining melted butter. Put them one on top of the other in a greased, round, ovenproof dish, letting the pastry edges fall over the side of the dish. Put the cubes of cod on the pastry, pour over the sauce and fold the edges of the pastry back over the filling. Brush the top with the remaining butter and bake for 15 minutes, until the cod is cooked.

Heat the butter and wine and sauté the mushrooms in the mixture until softened. Stir in the cream and season to taste. Transfer to a warmed serving bowl.

Serve the fish pie straight from the oven, from the cooking dish, and hand round the mushroom sauce separately.

READY STEADY COOK Tips

If your sauce goes lumpy while you are adding the milk, take it off the heat and whisk it thoroughly until all the lumps have gone. Then return it to a gentle heat and stir well until cooked.

You can substitute any firm-fleshed white fish for this recipe: try roughy or ling.

If you can buy some wild mushrooms and sauté them lightly to serve with the dish.

KEVIN WOODFORD

SARAH'S MEDLEY OF FRESH FISH ON A BED OF CHABLIS AND SPRING ONION SAUCE

Poached fish with a simple *beurre blanc* sauce, served with herb and prawn croûtons, carrots and spring onions

Sarah's last attempt at fish had been a tuna lasagne, which had ended up on the floor, so she definitely needed some help with cooking simple fish dishes.

SERVES 2
FOR THE CROÛTONS
1 small baguette
Handful of fresh coriander
Handful of fresh parsley
Handful of fresh dill
2 tablespoons olive oil
75 g (3 oz) cooked, peeled prawns
75 g (3 oz) shell-on cooked prawns

FOR THE FISH MEDLEY
175 ml (6 fl oz) water
5 carrots, cut into batons, trimmings reserved
Bunch of spring onions, green tops reserved
3 tablespoons Chablis or other white wine

200 g (7 oz) cod fillet, skin reserved and cut lengthways in half
200 g (7 oz) huss, bone removed, cut lengthways in half
$^1/_2$ lemon, sliced

FOR THE SAUCE
50 g (2 oz) unsalted butter, cubed
3 tablespoons double cream

TO GARNISH
4 tomatoes, skinned, halved, seeded and chopped
1 slice of lemon
Chopped fresh parsley

Make the croûtons first. Pre-heat the grill. Slice half the baguette and toast both sides of the slices. Roughly chop the remaining baguette. Chop enough coriander leaves to make a tablespoon of chopped herb and set aside. Put the chopped bread, whole coriander leaves, parsley, dill, oil and peeled prawns in a food processor and process to a smooth paste. Divide and spread on each slice of toasted baguette.

42

Put the water in a shallow saucepan, add some of the carrot trimmings, the spring onion tops, chopped coriander, wine, fish skins and lemon slices and simmer for about 4 minutes (remove the fish skins after the first minute). Add the huss and cod and cover the pan with a circle of greaseproof paper, if you don't have a lid. Poach for 4 minutes. Remove the fish and keep it warm.

To make the sauce, strain the stock through a fine nylon sieve and reduce it for 2 minutes. Add the butter and cream, stirring constantly until the sauce thickens.

Meanwhile, cook the carrots in salted, boiling water for 6 minutes, add the whole spring onions and cook for 2–3 minutes more. Drain.

To serve, arrange the herb and prawn croûtons on warmed serving plates and put the fish in the middle. Pour the sauce over the fish and garnish with a shell-on prawn, tomatoes, a curled lemon slice and chopped fresh parsley. Serve the carrots and spring onions to the side.

READY STEADY COOK Tips

To skin tomatoes, make a slit in the top of each and put them in a bowl. Pour on boiling water to cover and leave for 10 seconds. Drain and remove the skins, which will peel away easily from the slit. Remove seeds with a teaspoon. Cut away core with a sharp knife and chop the flesh.

When poaching fish, keep the heat very low so that the liquid just scarcely bubbles on the surface. Never overcook the fish or you will lose the tender, succulent texture.

To store fresh parsley, wash the sprigs and pat them dry. Place them in a polythene bag, tied very loosely, and store in the bottom of the fridge for a few days.

POULTRY AND GAME

LESLEY WATERS

RED HOT AND SPICY

Spicy turkey Stroganoff, turkey escalopes in dill sauce and courgette rice

Lorry driver Abdul had recently broken his leg during a rugby match and had become addicted to watching *Ready Steady Cook* from his sick bed. He told Lesley that he loved his food and especially loved it hot. This spicy turkey stroganoff could be as hot as you like, depending on the curry powder you use.

SERVES 3–4
6 x 100 g (4 oz) turkey breast steaks
FOR THE TURKEY STROGANOFF
2 tablespoons sunflower oil
$\frac{1}{2}$ onion, chopped
1 tablespoon curry powder
1 teaspoon ground turmeric
1 red pepper, seeded and sliced
2 tablespoons white wine
150 ml (5 fl oz) chicken stock
2 tablespoons tomato purée

FOR THE ESCALOPES
1 tablespoon olive oil
15 g ($\frac{1}{2}$ oz) butter
$\frac{1}{2}$ onion, chopped

1 tablespoon plain flour
4 tablespoons white wine
Grated zest and juice of 1 large orange
150 ml (5 fl oz) double cream
2 tablespoons chopped fresh dill
Salt and freshly ground black pepper

FOR THE RICE
200 g (7 oz) long-grain rice
25 g (1 oz) butter
1 large courgette, chopped
1 teaspoon ground turmeric
1 tablespoon chopped fresh coriander
1 tablespoon chopped fresh parsley
Salt and freshly ground black pepper
Dill sprigs, to garnish

Cook the rice in plenty of salted water, until tender. Drain and reserve. Meanwhile, slice three of the turkey steaks in thin strips. Heat the oil in a large frying-pan and sauté the onion, until soft. Add the curry powder and turmeric and fry for 30 seconds. Stir in the pepper and turkey and stir-fry for 3 minutes. Add the wine, stock and tomato purée and cook until the turkey is cooked through (no longer pink in the middle).

For the escalopes, heat the oil in another frying-pan and add the butter. Sauté the onion, until softened.

Put the other three turkey steaks between two sheets of cling film and beat them with a rolling-pin, to flatten them. Put the flour on a plate and season it. Dip the turkey in the flour to coat both sides. Add to the pan with the onion and fry for 3–4 minutes on each side. Add the wine, orange zest and juice and simmer for a minute. Stir in the cream and dill and season to taste. Bubble over a high heat for 1 minute and add a splash of water or stock if the sauce is too thick.

Melt the butter in a large pan and gently sauté the courgette for 2 minutes. Add turmeric. Stir in the drained rice and herbs. Season well.

To serve both dishes, tip the rice into cups or ramekin dishes (one per person) and invert them on to warmed plates. The stroganoff or the escalopes can be served alongside this mound of rice, garnished with dill sprigs.

LESLEY WATERS

FOR PETE'S SAKE

Paella with chicken-stuffed roasted peppers

Peter Eblett admitted to being incredibly impatient in the kitchen and simply wanted to create something tasty in as little time as possible.

SERVES 4	350 g (12 oz) long-grain rice
FOR THE PAELLA	1 teaspoon ground turmeric
2 tablespoons olive oil	100 ml ($3^1/_2$ fl oz) white wine
1 onion, chopped	600 ml (1 pint) vegetable or chicken stock
1 fennel bulb, chopped	1 lime, grated rind and juice
2 garlic cloves, crushed	1 tablespoon chopped fresh parsley
450 g (1 lb) boneless, skinless chicken breast, cut in 1 cm ($1/_2$ in) cubes	Salt and freshly ground black pepper

FOR THE PEPPERS	FOR THE DRESSING
FOR THE PEPPERS	**FOR THE DRESSING**
1 red pepper, halved and seeded	3 tablespoons olive oil
1 green pepper, halved and seeded	2 tablespoons white-wine vinegar
2 tablespoons olive oil	2 tablespoons chopped fresh parsley
400 g (14 oz) tin of chopped tomatoes	1 teaspoon mustard
Salt and freshly ground black pepper	2 teaspoons water
	Salt and freshly ground black pepper

Pre-heat the oven to gas mark 6, 200°C, 400°F. Heat the oil in a pan, add the onion, three-quarters of the fennel, the garlic and half the chicken and season with salt and pepper. Cook for 4 minutes. Stir in the rice and turmeric and add the wine and stock. Cover and simmer for 10–15 minutes, until the liquid has been absorbed and the rice is tender. Check regularly and add more stock if it dries out.

Meanwhile, put the pepper halves, cut side down, on a baking sheet and brush them with a tablespoon of oil. Roast for 10 minutes.

Heat the remaining tablespoon of oil in a pan, add the rest of the fennel and chicken and cook for 4 minutes. Add the tomatoes, season and leave to simmer for 5 minutes.

Meanwhile, make the dressing. Put the oil in a bowl with the vinegar, parsley, mustard, water and salt and pepper. Whisk together and pour over the peppers.

Spoon the chicken and tomato mixture into the roasted peppers.

Stir the lime juice and rind into the paella, with the parsley. Transfer to warmed serving plates and serve with the roasted peppers.

LESLEY WATERS

BACKPACKERS' FEAST

Cinnamon-spiced chicken casserole with hoummos, served with couscous cooked with carrot and onion

As she was soon to be travelling around the world on a tight budget, Ruth Lloyd saw her fiver budget as a real challenge. She sped around her local supermarket, determined to buy as many ingredients as possible. And didn't she do well! Lesley rose magnificently to the occasion with this interesting combination of casserole, couscous and hoummos.

SERVES 2–3

FOR THE COUSCOUS
200 g (7 oz) couscous
1 tablespoon olive oil
½ onion, chopped
3 carrots, chopped
Coriander leaves, to garnish

FOR THE CASSEROLE
2 tablespoons olive oil
½ onion, chopped
375 g (13 oz) skinless, boneless chicken thighs, cut in strips
2 teaspoons ground cinnamon
2 garlic cloves, crushed
1 aubergine, cubed

1 courgette, cubed
2 tablespoons tomato purée
200 ml (7 fl oz) white wine
200 ml (7 fl oz) chicken stock or water

FOR THE HOUMMOS
400 g (14 oz) tin of chick-peas, rinsed and drained
150 ml (5 fl oz) Greek yoghurt
1 garlic clove, crushed
2 tablespoons chopped fresh coriander
1 orange, halved
Olive oil
Salt and freshly ground black pepper
Coriander leaves, to garnish

Soak the couscous in plenty of boiling water for 10 minutes. Strain through a sieve, place the sieve over a large pan of simmering water, cover and leave to steam for 6–10 minutes.

Meanwhile, make the casserole. Heat the oil in a large pan and sauté the onion for 3 minutes, until softened. Add the chicken and cook, stirring, until sealed on all sides. Add the cinnamon, garlic, aubergine and courgette, stirring constantly. Add the tomato purée and wine and leave to cook for 15–20 minutes, stirring occasionally and adding a little water or chicken stock if necessary.

To garnish the couscous, heat the oil in a pan, add the onion and the carrots and cook slowly for 4–5 minutes until tender.

For the hommos, put half the chick-peas into a blender or food processor, with the yoghurt, garlic and coriander, and the juice of half the orange. Blend or process to a soft consistency. Season to taste.

Cut the remaining half-orange into segments, spoon the hommos on to a serving plate and spoon the reserved chick-peas and orange segments round the outside. Drizzle over a little olive oil, sprinkle with a little pepper and a few fresh coriander leaves, to garnish.

Tip the couscous out of the sieve on to a plate in a mound, spoon the cooked carrot and onion on top and garnish with coriander. Serve the casserole in a dish.

L E S L E Y   W A T E R S

MACCLESFIELD TEX MEX

Turkey chilli with tortillas, with turkey patties

Rugby-playing Peter Ord was fed up with the boring food he and the lads were being served after matches and wanted an idea for something more exciting: 'It's especially important if we lose ... again'. Chilli con carne made with turkey mince was definitely a winning tackle.

SERVES 2
FOR THE CHILLI
1 tablespoon olive oil
$^1/_2$ onion, finely chopped
350 g (12 oz) turkey mince
1 teaspoon ground cumin
1 teaspoon flour
2 teaspoons paprika
1 teaspoon tomato purée

3 tablespoons red wine
300 ml (10 fl oz) chicken stock
$^1/_2$ Habanero or small red chilli, seeded and finely chopped
Salt and freshly ground black pepper

FOR THE PATTIES
Slice of white country-style bread
1 tablespoon roughly chopped fresh coriander

½ Habanero or small red chilli, seeded
1 egg yolk
1 tablespoon olive oil

FOR THE DRESSING
3 tablespoons olive oil
1 tablespoon lemon juice
1 tablespoon chopped fresh coriander
½ Habanero or small red chilli, seeded
and finely chopped

TO SERVE
6 flour tortillas
2 tablespoons olive oil
½ onion, sliced
½ Iceberg lettuce, roughly sliced
1 orange, peel and pith removed
and thinly sliced
4 tablespoons Greek yoghurt

Pre-heat the oven to gas mark 6, 200°C, 400°F. Heat the oil in a frying-pan and add the onion. Cook for 3 minutes, or until softened. Then add three-quarters of the turkey mince, the cumin, flour, paprika, tomato purée, wine, stock and chilli and simmer for 8–10 minutes, or until the turkey is cooked and saucy. Add extra stock if necessary. Season with salt and pepper and keep warm.

Meanwhile, make the patties. Put the bread in a food processor and process for 10 seconds. Add the remaining turkey mince and process for 10 seconds. Add the coriander, half-chilli and egg yolk and process until mixed thoroughly. Mould the mixture into six small patties. Heat a frying-pan with the olive oil. Fry the patties for 3–5 minutes on each side, or until golden.

Place the tortillas on a baking sheet and bake for 3 minutes, to warm through.

Meanwhile, in a bowl mix the ingredients for the dressing. Keep to one side.

In a wok, heat the olive oil. Cut two of the tortillas into strips and, when the oil is smoking, stir-fry the tortilla strips and onion slices for about 2 minutes.

To assemble, put the lettuce and orange slices on a plate with the patties. Drizzle over the dressing and scatter the tortilla strips on top. On a separate plate, put a warmed tortilla. Spread on some of the turkey chilli and drizzle over the Greek yoghurt. Repeat with the remaining tortillas. Serve at once.

LESLEY WATERS

THAI-FRY

Stir-fried chicken noodles, served with chinese-leaf salad
with peanut sauce

Glenn from Rotherham told us there were two things he loved to do at the weekends:
one was cooking and the other was wallpapering his caravan! Fern and Lesley decided
to stick to cooking!

SERVES 2

FOR THE NOODLES

85 g (3oz) packet of instant rice noodles
1 boneless, skinless chicken breast, weighing
about 225 g (8 oz), sliced
1 tablespoon vegetable oil
1 fresh red chilli, seeded and
cut in small pieces
150 g (5 oz) beansprouts
2 spring onions, green tops only
Salt and freshly ground black pepper

FOR THE MARINADE

1 lime, cut in small pieces
1 teaspoon sesame oil
1 teaspoon soy sauce
2 tablespoons chopped fresh coriander
1 garlic clove, crushed

FOR THE OMELETTE

1 tablespoon sunflower oil
3 eggs
1 tablespoon chopped fresh coriander

FOR THE SALAD

1 small head of Chinese leaves, shredded
2 carrots, peeled into strips
2 teaspoons soy sauce
1 teaspoon sesame oil
Salt and freshly ground black pepper

FOR THE SAUCE

50 g (2 oz) unsalted skinned peanuts
1 tablespoon chopped fresh coriander
3 tablespoons water
1 teaspoon soy sauce
1 tablespoon Thai fish sauce, to taste
75 ml (3 fl oz) sunflower oil
Chopped fresh parsley
1 tablespoon lemon juice
Salt and freshly ground black pepper

TO SERVE

1 orange, peeled and sliced
2 spring onions, green tops only,
roughly chopped

Put the noodles in a large, deep pan or bowl, fill with boiling water and leave to soak for 6–10 minutes, or according to the packet instructions. Drain thoroughly.

Meanwhile, marinade the chicken in a bowl, with the lime pieces, sesame oil, soy sauce, coriander and garlic.

For the omelette, heat the oil in a non-stick fryng-pan. Lightly whisk the eggs in a bowl. Season and add the coriander. Pour into the frying-pan and make an omelette. To cook the other side, invert on to a plate and put back into the pan. Cook for 1–2 minutes. Tip on to a board, cool slightly, roll up and cut in strips.

In a bowl, put three-quarters of the Chinese leaves, the carrots, soy sauce and sesame oil. Toss together, season and leave to one side.

Now finish the noodles. Heat the oil in a wok and stir-fry the chicken with the marinade for 4–5 minutes, or until cooked. Add the reserved Chinese leaves, the chilli, beansprouts, half the green tops of the spring onions, the omelette and noodles. Season and toss together until heated through.

To make the peanut sauce, put three-quarters of the peanuts into a food processor, with the coriander, water, soy sauce and fish sauce. Process until smooth and, with the motor still running, slowly pour in the oil. Stir in some parsley and the lemon juice. Check and adjust the seasoning.

Serve the stir-fried noodles on a plate. Garnish with the remaining spring onions and reserved peanuts. Arrange the salad and the orange slices to the side and drizzle on some of the peanut sauce.

BOBBY'S BURGER SURPRISE

Turkey burgers with honey-roasted parsnips and kumquat marmalade

Bobby Hoyle wanted to surprise her dad with a special meal for Christmas. Much to his relief Kevin did most of the cooking as, since her seventh birthday, when he bought her a junior cookbook, she's been inflicting experiments – and disasters – from the kitchen on him.

SERVES 2

FOR THE PARSNIPS
1 tablespoon olive oil
15 g ($^1/_2$ oz) butter
1 tablespoon clear honey
8 baby parsnips, topped and tailed
1 tablespoon finely chopped fresh parsley
1 tablespoon finely chopped fresh coriander
Salt and freshly ground black pepper

FOR THE BURGERS
5 slices of white bread
Chopped fresh parsley
225 g (8 oz) turkey mince
2 rashers of bacon, chopped
2 garlic cloves, finely chopped
1 egg, beaten
Salt and freshly ground black pepper

TO COAT THE BURGERS
75 g (3 oz) plain flour
2 eggs, lightly beaten
1 tablespoon olive oil

FOR THE MARMALADE
40 g ($1^1/_2$ oz) butter
1 large onion, roughly chopped
1 garlic clove, finely chopped
150 g (5 oz) kumquats, sliced
2 tablespoons chopped fresh parsley
75 ml (3 fl oz) brandy
3 tablespoons cranberry sauce
Tabasco sauce

FOR THE CARROTS
6 baby carrots
Butter

TO GARNISH
Sage and dill sprigs

Pre-heat the oven to gas mark 6, 200°C, 400°F. Heat the oil and butter in an ovenproof pan, add the honey, toss in the parsnips and season, sprinkle the parsley and coriander on top, transfer to the oven and bake for 15–18 minutes.

Meanwhile, make the burgers. Put the bread in a food processor and blend into breadcrumbs. Add a handful of the parsley and blend in. Put the mince in a bowl, with the bacon and garlic, add the egg and a handful of breadcrumbs, mix together and season. Prepare a plate of seasoned flour, a plate of breadcrumbs and a shallow bowl of beaten egg. Take a ball of the turkey mince and coat it in flour, dip it in the egg and finally in the breadcrumbs. Flatten into a burger shape. Heat the oil in a frying-pan, put the burgers in and cook over a medium heat for about 5–6 minutes each side, or until cooked in the centre and golden brown.

For the hot marmalade, heat the butter in another frying-pan, add the onion and garlic and cook until softened. Add the kumquats and some parsley. Pour in the brandy and flambé, tilting and rotating the pan until the flames die down. Add the cranberry sauce and a couple of drops of Tabasco sauce and cook for a further 3–4 minutes.

Boil the carrots until tender. Drain, return to the pan and toss with a knob of butter, to glaze.

To serve, place the burgers on a plate, spoon the kumquat mixture on to the side, surround with the parsnips and carrots and garnish with dill and sage.

READY STEADY COOK Tips

Warm the brandy in the pan for a few seconds before you flambé it to enhance the flavour. If you are using gas, tilt the pan slightly to ignite the brandy. Otherwise use a taper. Let the alcohol burn off and the flames will then die down on their own.

Leave a little of the trimmed green stalks on the baby carrots for an attractive effect.

DISCIPLINED DUCK

Crisp-griddled duck with savoury rice, sweet and sour sauce, stir-fried vegetables and 'seaweed'

Working in a police complaints and discipline department, Jim Smith needed something special to impress 'the lads'.

SERVES 2

FOR THE RICE
25 g (1 oz) butter
1 garlic clove, crushed
4 spring onions, chopped
100 g (4 oz) long-grain rice
300 ml (10 fl oz) boiling water
2 eggs, beaten

FOR THE MARINADE
1 tablespoon white-wine vinegar
1 tablespoon honey
Tabasco sauce
juice of ½ orange
2 teaspoon chopped fresh coriander
1 garlic clove, crushed
2 boneless duck breasts
Salt and freshly ground black pepper

FOR THE SAUCE
4 teaspoons white-wine vinegar
2 tablespoons tomato ketchup
2 teaspoons brown sugar

FOR THE VEGETABLES
1 tablespoon vegetable oil
1 small onion, chopped
1 red pepper, seeded and sliced
1 courgette, thinly sliced

FOR THE 'SEAWEED'
6 tablespoons vegetable oil
250 g (9 oz) spring greens, finely shredded
Salt and freshly ground black pepper
Coriander leaves, to garnish

Pre-heat the oven to gas mark 7, 220°C, 425°F. Melt the butter in a pan and add the garlic, spring onions and rice. Cook together for 2 minutes before adding the water; reduce the heat and leave to simmer for 10–12 minutes, or until tender and most of the water has been absorbed. Add more water as necessary during cooking.

To make the marinade, in a bowl, mix together the vinegar, honey, a few drops of Tabasco sauce, the orange juice, coriander and garlic and season with salt and pepper. Add the duck and leave to marinate for a few minutes while you heat a griddle pan. Griddle the duck, skin-side down, for 4 minutes, until the skin is crisp. Transfer to the oven and continue cooking for 10–15 minutes.

Meanwhile, make the sauce. Into a small pan, put the vinegar, tomato ketchup and sugar and simmer together for 1–2 minutes, adding a little water to make a smooth sauce.

For the stir-fried vegetables, heat the oil and stir-fry the onion, pepper and courgette for 2–3 minutes.

For the 'seaweed', heat the remaining oil in a wok and stir-fry the shredded spring greens for 4–5 minutes, until crisp but still green and season. Drain on kitchen paper.

Stir the eggs into the rice and heat through. Do not overheat as the mixture will curdle. To serve, carve the duck into slices. Put a bed of rice on two warmed serving plates. Spoon the stir-fried vegetables on to the rice and arrange the slices of duck and 'seaweed' on top. Keep warm. Pour the duck cooking juices into the sauce and heat through. Then pour the sauce round the rice and garnish the dish with coriander leaves.

KEVIN WOODFORD

NAN'S CELEBRATION RABBIT

Rabbit casserole with herby dumplings and orange leeks

Nan Bourne was invited along to our VE Day show as she had been in the fire service during the war, driving mobile canteens and manning the pumps. A further cause for celebration was the fact that her 55th wedding anniversary was just two weeks away.

SERVES 2	1 rabbit, cut into chunks and small sharp
FOR THE CASSEROLE	bones removed
2 tablespoons sunflower oil	2 carrots, sliced

1 tablespoon chopped fresh parsley
1 tablespoon chopped fresh coriander
1 tablespoon chopped fresh mint
1 tablespoon plain flour
1 tablespoon tomato purée
300 ml (10 fl oz) red wine
1 potato, peeled and cut into balls *à la Parisienne* or chopped
Salt and freshly ground black pepper

FOR THE LEEKS
3 leeks, cut in 1 cm (¹/₂ in) slices

25 g (1 oz) butter
Juice of 1 orange
Salt and freshly ground black pepper

FOR THE DUMPLINGS
50 g (2 oz) self-raising flour
25 g (1 oz) vegetable suet
1 tablespoon chopped fresh parsley
2 tablespoons chopped fresh coriander
1 tablespoon chopped fresh mint
2 tablespoons water
Salt and freshly ground black pepper

To make the rabbit casserole, heat the oil in heavy-based frying-pan and brown the rabbit pieces, carrots and parsley, coriander and mint. Stir in the flour and tomato purée and cook for a further minute. Then pour in the wine, stirring continuously, and bring to the boil. The sauce should thicken. Add the potato balls and let the rabbit simmer for 12–15 minutes, until the rabbit is cooked (the juices should run clear). Season to taste.

Sauté the leeks in the butter for 4 minutes, stirring occasionally. Add the orange juice, season and cook for a further 2–3 minutes.

For the dumplings, mix the flour, suet and seasoning with the herbs and water, to form a sticky mixture. Shape into little balls and cook in a pan of simmering water for 5 minutes.

To serve, spoon the rabbit casserole on to two warmed plates and arrange the dumplings around the edge. Serve the leeks separately.

READY STEADY COOK Tip
If you don't like rabbit, try this idea with chicken portions. They will need to be cooked in the casserole for at least 30 minutes, depending on size. Check that they are cooked through, by piercing the thickest part with a skewer; the juices should be clear, not pink, and the flesh should be white.

KEVIN WOODFORD

HEAVEN ON EARTH

Chicken breast stuffed with apricots, pepper and chicory salad, spicy rice and cucumber salad

Rita Chada from Birmingham named her dish Heaven on Earth, not only because it tasted delicious but also because cooking without her 'clumsy and useless in the kitchen' husband certainly did feel like heaven!

SERVES 2

FOR THE RICE
100 g (4 oz) long-grain rice
1 garlic clove, crushed
2 teaspoons garam masala

FOR THE CHICKEN
1 shallot, chopped
1 button mushroom, sliced
1/2 small red pepper, seeded and chopped
25 g (1 oz) butter
6 canned apricot halves in natural juice, sliced
2 boneless, skinless chicken breasts
1 chicken stock cube, dissolved in

600 ml (1 pint) boiling water
Salt and freshly ground black pepper

FOR THE CUCUMBER SALAD
2 tablespoons Greek yoghurt
1/2 cucumber, sliced
2 tablespoons chopped fresh mint

FOR THE SALAD
1 small oak-leaf lettuce
1/2 red pepper, seeded and chopped
1 head of chicory
2 teaspoons medium curry powder
125 ml (4 fl oz) good-quality mayonnaise
Salt and freshly ground black pepper

Pre-heat the oven to gas mark 7, 220°C, 425°F. Cook the rice in salted, boiling water, with the crushed garlic and the garam masala, according to the instructions on the packet.

Sauté the shallot, mushroom and red pepper in the butter for 5 minutes and season. Add the apricots and continue cooking for 2 minutes. Flatten each chicken breast with a rolling-pin between two sheets of cling film to a thickness of 5 mm (¼ in). Spoon half the mushroom and pepper mixture on to each chicken breast. Roll up each breast and lightly wrap each one in foil. Put the rolled chicken in an ovenproof dish, with the stock and cook for 15 minutes, until the chicken is cooked and no longer pink. Unwrap, allow the rolls to cool slightly and carefully slice each breast into four or five.

To make the cucumber salad, mix the yoghurt with the cucumber and mint.

For the salad, arrange the lettuce, red pepper and chicory leaves on each plate. Mix the curry powder into the mayonnaise and, if necessary, thin it slightly with a tablespoon of water and season.

To serve, arrange the chicken slices on a bed of the rice and spoon the mayonnaise over the chicken. Serve on the same plate as the cucumber and salad.

K E V I N   W O O D F O R D

BURFORD QUAIL

Casseroled quail in red wine, with shredded sprouts
and sweet-potato mash

Wendy fancied challenging Kevin to something a bit unusual and tipped a quail from her bag, grinning from ear to ear. She told us that she was always happy 'which annoys my grumpy husband intensely'.

SERVES 2
FOR THE CASSEROLE
2 tablespoons oil
1 onion, roughly chopped
3 celery sticks, roughly chopped
1 leek, sliced
2 quails
450 ml (15 fl oz) red wine

FOR THE SWEET-POTATO MASH
450 g (1 lb) sweet potato, peeled and cubed

15 g (1/2 oz) butter
Salt and freshly ground black pepper

FOR THE BRUSSELS SPROUTS
350 g (12 oz) Brussels sprouts
1 tablespoon olive oil
Salt and freshly ground black pepper

FOR THE *BEURRE MANIÉ*
15 g (1/2 oz) butter, softened
15 g (1/2 oz) plain flour

59

Heat the oil in a pan, add the onion, celery and leek and cook until softened. Add the quail and seal until well browned. Pour in the wine, making sure the liquid covers the quail. Cover with a lid and simmer at just below boiling point for 15 minutes, turning the quail halfway through cooking.

Meanwhile, boil the sweet-potatoes in salted water for 10 minutes. Drain and add a knob of butter. Season with salt and pepper and then mash well.

Peel the outer layer from the sprouts, cut off the stems and grate the remainder. Heat the oil in a frying-pan, add the sprouts, season and fry gently for 3–4 minutes, until slightly softened.

Make the *beurre manié* by kneading the butter in a bowl with your fingers and working in the flour. Remove the quail from the pan and keep warm. Stir the *beurre manié* a little at a time into the red wine stock, to thicken it.

Arrange the vegetables on two warmed plates, put the quails on top and pour over the thickened red-wine sauce.

READY STEADY COOK Tips

Beurre manié *means 'kneaded butter'. It is a good way to thicken all kinds of sauces and casseroles at the end of cooking, giving a rich and shiny appearance.*

If you don't want to use quail or another kind of game bird in this recipe, try it with a small chicken or poussin, halved, or chicken portions.

POSTMASTER PETE'S DUCKLING

Golden duck legs with parsnip sauce, saffron rice and sesame broccoli

Peter Dimaline, from Doncaster, claimed that he'd 'kill for duck' and wanted a dish that included masses of ginger; he's generally deprived of his favourite flavouring, because his wife hates it!

SERVES 2

FOR THE DUCK
2 x 225 g (8 oz) duckling legs, boned
2 parsley sprigs
2 teaspoons wholegrain mustard
1 tablespoon sunflower oil
Salt and freshly ground black pepper

FOR THE SAUCE
225 g (8 oz) parsnips, cut in 2 cm ($^3/_4$ in) cubes
1 teaspoon mustard
2 teaspoons clear honey
1 cm ($^1/_2$ in) piece of fresh root ginger, peeled and finely chopped
1 tablespoon chopped fresh parsley
Juice of 2 limes
150 ml (5 fl oz) red wine
Salt and freshly ground black pepper

FOR THE RICE
1 tablespoon sunflower oil
2 shallots or 1 small onion, finely chopped
100 g (4 oz) long-grain rice
Pinch of saffron threads
450 ml (15 fl oz) water
Salt and freshly ground black pepper

FOR THE BROCCOLI
1 tablespoon sunflower oil
225 g (8 oz) broccoli, cut in small florets
2 garlic cloves, crushed
1 tablespoon sesame seeds
15 g ($^1/_2$ oz) butter
Salt and freshly ground black pepper

TO GARNISH
Slices of lime
Flatleaf parsley sprigs

Pre-heat the oven to gas mark 6, 200°C, 400°F. Season the duckling legs, put a sprig of parsley in the centre of each and then roll up and secure with kitchen string. Spread a teaspoon of mustard over each duckling roll. Heat the oil in a frying-pan and fry the duckling for 5 minutes, turning until golden. Transfer to a baking tray and bake for 12–15 minutes.

Meanwhile, cook the parsnips in a pan of salted, boiling water for 8–10 minutes until tender.

For the rice, heat the oil in a pan, add the shallots or onion and cook for a minute. Stir in the rice, saffron and seasoning and then add the water. Bring to the boil and cook for 8–10 minutes, until the rice is tender.

Drain and mash the parsnips. Stir in the mustard, honey, ginger, parsley, lime juice, wine and seasoning. Simmer for 5 minutes, until the sauce has reduced slightly.

Heat the oil in a frying-pan, add the broccoli, garlic and sesame seeds and season with salt and pepper. Stir-fry for 2 minutes. Stir in the butter and cook for a minute.

Spoon the rice into two 10 cm (4 in) ramekin dishes and press down lightly.

To serve, turn the rice out on to two warmed serving plates. Arrange a duckling leg next to the rice. Spoon over the parsnip sauce and garnish with slices of lime and sprigs of flatleaf parsley. Serve with the sesame broccoli.

READY STEADY COOK Tips

Flatleaf parsley has a fuller flavour than the more common curled parsley, although this is fine to use instead if you do not have the continental variety.

Cut the broccoli in even-sized florets so that they all cook in the same amount of time to a tender but slightly crisp finish.

Freshly squeezed lime juice is the best thing to use, but you can now buy bottled lime juice, which is handy to have in the fridge to pep up your cooking.

MEAT DISHES

LESLEY WATERS

PIG OUT

Sliced white hog's pudding, with warm potato salad and sweet and sour red cabbage

Never having tried white hog's pudding before, Jim Cribbett was more than happy to 'pig out' on this hearty meal.

SERVES 2–4

FOR THE POTATOES
100 g (4 oz) new potatoes, halved lengthways
2 tablespoons olive oil

FOR THE CABBAGE
2 tablespoons olive oil
1 baby red cabbage, sliced
150 ml (5 fl oz) red wine
$1\frac{1}{2}$ tablespoons caster sugar
1 teaspoon red-wine vinegar
225 g (8 oz) spring greens, shredded
150 g (5 oz) pancetta, cubed

FOR THE PUDDING
2 tablespoons olive oil
225 g (8 oz) white hog's pudding, or black pudding, sliced thickly
1 red onion, sliced
1 green apple, cored and sliced

FOR THE DRESSING
1 tablespoon balsamic vinegar
1 tablespoon olive oil
1 tablespoon chopped fresh rosemary
Salt and freshly ground black pepper

Cook the potatoes in boiling, salted water, until tender.
   Heat the oil in a frying-pan and cook the red cabbage for 4 minutes. Add the wine, sugar and vinegar and continue cooking for a further 4 minutes until just tender.
   Blanch the spring greens in boiling, salted water for a minute. Refresh under cold water and set to one side.
   Add the cubed pancetta to the cabbage and season with salt and ground black pepper.
   Heat the oil in a frying-pan and fry the hog's pudding slices for 2 minutes on each side. Add the onion and apple and cook for 3–4 minutes or until golden.

MEAT DISHES

Heat another pan with the 2 tablespoons of oil. Add the potatoes and fry until golden and crisp.

Mix together the dressing ingredients, season and pour over the potatoes.

Heat a little oil in a wok and tip in the greens, just to warm through.

Divide the cabbage and greens between warmed serving plates. Arrange the hog's pudding slices around the outside, with the apples and onions and the potatoes.

LESLEY WATERS

CAROLE'S KEBABS

Minced lamb kebabs with vegetables in wine, spinach and orange salad and creamed spinach

Carole came on the show with a mission. 'Please show me something interesting to do with mince', she begged. Lesley obliged with these Middle-Eastern-style minced-meat kebabs.

SERVES 2

FOR THE KEBABS
450 g (1 lb) minced lamb or beef
1 tablespoon ground cumin
1 tablespoon ground coriander
2 teaspoons dried oregano
1 egg white
1 tablespoon olive oil
Salt and freshly ground black pepper

FOR THE VEGETABLES
2 tablespoon olive oil
1 onion, sliced
1 fennel bulb, cut in 5 cm (2 in) pieces
1 red pepper, seeded and sliced

1 medium potato, halved and thinly sliced
100 ml (4 fl oz) white wine

FOR THE CITRUS DRESSING
Juice of 1 lemon
2 oranges
3 tablespoons olive oil
Salt and freshly ground black pepper

FOR THE SPINACH
225 g (8 oz) fresh spinach, washed
2 tablespoons double cream
Pinch of grated nutmeg
Salt and freshly ground black pepper
2 tablespoons chopped fresh coriander, to garnish

65

Pre-heat the oven to gas mark 8, 230°C, 450°F or pre-heat the grill to hot. Put the lamb, cumin, coriander, oregano and egg white in a bowl. Season with salt and pepper and mix thoroughly with your hands. Divide the mixture into four and shape into sausages around oiled kebab skewers. Wrap the ends of the skewers in foil, put them on a baking tray and drizzle the oil over the kebabs. Cook for 10–12 minutes, until the vegetables are tender, turning occasionally.

For the vegetables, heat the oil in a pan and cook the onion for 5 minutes. Add the fennel, pepper and potato and cook for 8–10 minutes. Add the wine and cook for 3–4 minutes.

Put the lemon juice and juice of one orange in a bowl with the oil and season with salt and pepper. Cut all the peel and white pith off the second orange and slice it thinly. Toss half the spinach, the orange slices and half of the citrus dressing together.

Put the remaining spinach in a pan, with just the water that clings to its leaves, and cook for 2 minutes, until wilted. Stir in the cream, nutmeg and seasoning and cook for a minute.

To serve, put the mixed vegetables on two warmed plates and drizzle over the rest of the citrus dressing. Remove the foil and put the kebabs on top, sprinkle over the chopped coriander. Serve with the creamed spinach and the spinach and orange salad.

LESLEY WATERS

GOULASH AND MASH

Beef goulash with mashed potatoes and spiced fried bread

With winter approaching thick and fast, Alistair Burns wanted a heartwarming dish to see him through the cold months.

SERVES 2	15 g (¹/₂ oz) butter
FOR THE MASH	3 tablespoons milk
450 g (1 lb) potatoes, cut in	225 g (8 oz) Greek yoghurt
1 cm (¹/₂ in) cubes	

2 tablespoons roughly chopped fresh parsley
Salt and freshly ground black pepper

FOR THE GOULASH
2 tablespoons olive oil
1 large onion, chopped
Pinch of sugar
1 green pepper, seeded and chopped
1 red pepper, seeded and chopped
2 tablespoons paprika
350 g (12 oz) stir-fry beef strips
Cayenne pepper

150 ml (5 fl oz) red wine
450 g (1 lb) tomatoes, roughly chopped
1 tablespoon lemon juice
1 bay leaf
150 ml (5 fl oz) vegetable or beef stock

FOR THE SPICED BREAD
50 g (2 oz) butter
1 tablespoon sunflower oil
1 teaspoon ground cumin
1 teaspoon paprika
2 thick slices of bread, cut in rough chunks

Cook the potatoes in a pan of salted, boiling water for 8–10 minutes, until tender.

Meanwhile, for the goulash, heat the oil in a large pan, add the onion and cook for 3 minutes. Add the green and red peppers and cook for 2 minutes. Stir in the paprika and cook for a minute more. Add the beef and a pinch of Cayenne pepper and season with salt, pepper and the sugar. Cook, stirring, for 2 minutes. Add the wine, tomatoes, lemon juice and bay leaf and simmer for 10 minutes, adding 3–4 tablespoons of stock if the sauce gets too thick. Remove the bay leaf.

Heat the butter and oil in a large frying-pan, add the cumin and paprika and cook for 30 seconds. Fry the bread in the spiced butter for 3–4 minutes, turning once and taking care not to burn the spices.

Drain the potatoes, add the butter and mash well. Mix in the milk, 4 tablespoons of the yoghurt, the parsley and seasoning.

Thin the rest of the yoghurt with 1–2 tablespoons of water. To serve, spoon the goulash on to a plate and serve with the mashed potatoes and spiced fried bread. Serve the yoghurt separately.

MOUTHWATERING MEDITERRANEAN MAGIC

Marinated lamb chops with garlic-mashed potatoes, ratatouille and aubergine

School teacher, Paul Caine, loves to get his pupils cooking and had recently turned the classroom into a French bistro. His pupils got revenge by sending him to the programme.

SERVES 2

FOR THE LAMB
1 lamb steak, halved, or 2 chump chops
1 tablespoon white wine
1 tablespoon olive oil
5–6 sage leaves, shredded
Salt and freshly ground black pepper

FOR THE RATATOUILLE
2 tablespoons olive oil
1 onion, chopped
1 garlic clove, roughly chopped
4 apricots, stoned and quartered
3 tablespoons white wine
5 tomatoes, roughly chopped
1 tablespoon tomato purée

10 pitted green olives, halved
Salt and freshly ground black pepper

FOR THE MASHED POTATOES
350 g (12 oz) potatoes, peeled and cubed
1 garlic clove, crushed
2 tablespoons basil, roughly chopped
2 tablespoons double cream
2 tablespoons milk
Salt and freshly ground black pepper

FOR THE AUBERGINE
1 aubergine, sliced thickly
Juice of 1 lemon
7 tablespoons olive oil
Salt and freshly ground black pepper

Marinate the lamb in the wine, oil, sage and salt and pepper for at least 10 minutes (if time, for 1–2 hours).

To make the ratatouille, heat the oil and sweat the onion for a few minutes, until it is soft and translucent. Add the garlic and sauté for a minute. Then add the apricots and continue to cook for 3–4 minutes. Stir in the wine, tomatoes, and tomato purée, season with salt and black pepper and simmer for 10 minutes. Then stir in the olives.

For the mashed potatoes, boil the potatoes in salted, boiling water for 12–15 minutes. Drain and mash the potatoes with the garlic, basil, cream and milk. Season. For a milder taste, fry the garlic for 30 seconds in a little oil and butter, before adding it to the potatoes.

Pre-heat the barbecue or grill. Soak the aubergine slices for 5 minutes in the lemon juice, salt and pepper and 5 tablespoons of the oil. Then fry the aubergine with the marinade in the remaining 2 tablespoons of oil for 5 minutes. Grill the lamb for 5–6 minutes on each side.

To serve, put the aubergines on warmed plates. Arrange the lamb on top, with the ratatouille on the side and serve with the potatoes.

KEVIN WOODFORD

AUBERGINE MAGGLIACCIO

Aubergines stuffed with creamy pork, with saffron rice

Pauline was married to an Italian whose mother was a fantastic cook, so she was desperate for Kevin to give her some tips to impress her man with

SERVES 2

FOR THE AUBERGINES
25 g (1 oz) butter
1 tablespoon oil
225 g (8 oz) pork fillet, trimmed and cut in 1 cm ($\frac{1}{2}$ in) cubes
1 aubergine
3 spring onions, chopped
1 dessert apple, peeled, cored and chopped
1 tablespoon snipped fresh chives
1 tablespoon chopped fresh coriander
1 tablespoon chopped fresh parsley
2 tablespoons Dijon mustard

90 ml (3 fl oz) white wine
2 tablespoons double cream
2 tablespoons grated parmesan cheese
Salt and freshly ground black pepper

FOR THE RICE
1 tablespoon oil
2 spring onions, chopped
1 garlic clove, crushed
100 g (4 oz) long-grain rice
Pinch of saffron threads
$\frac{1}{2}$ chicken stock cube, dissolved in 300 ml (10 fl oz) boiling water

Heat the butter and oil in a frying-pan and fry the pork for 2 minutes. Cut the aubergine in half lengthways, spoon out the flesh and chop it. Keep the shells. Add the aubergine flesh, spring onions, apple and herbs to the frying-pan and season with salt and pepper. Continue cooking for 3 minutes. Stir in the mustard and wine and bring to the boil. Turn down the heat and simmer until the pork is almost cooked. Mix in the cream and parmesan cheese and continue to cook until the sauce has thickened. Meanwhile, pre-heat the grill to hot.

Pile the pork mixture into the aubergine skins and place under the pre-heated grill for 8 minutes.

Meanwhile, make the rice. Sauté the spring onions in the oil until softened. Add the garlic and rice and sauté for 1–2 minutes, until the rice grains are well coated in oil. Stir in the saffron and the stock. Reduce the heat and cook until the rice has absorbed the liquid. When the rice is cooked, spoon it into two ramekins.

To serve, put the stuffed aubergine halves on two warmed plates. Turn out the rice so it forms a small, neat mound next to the aubergine.

LESLEY WATERS

TONE'S POT BELLY PORK

Marinated belly pork with spiced red cabbage with apple and garlic roast potatoes

Tone from Staffordshire had but one plea for Lesley: 'Can you give my red cabbage some "oomph"?' This spicy cabbage mixture is slightly sweet and sour and packs a real flavour punch, enough to make it a robust partner for garlicky potatoes and marinated belly of pork.

SERVES 2
FOR THE MARINADE
2 teaspoons Worcestershire sauce
4 teaspoons soy sauce
2 1/2 tablespoons clear honey

2 teaspoons tomato purée
A few drops of Tabasco sauce
1 teaspoon dried mixed herbs
3 teaspoons wholegrain mustard
Sprig of fresh rosemary

MEAT DISHES

FOR THE PORK
300 g (11 oz) belly pork, cut in two
1 tablespoon olive oil
2 tablespoons red wine

FOR THE POTATOES
2 medium potatoes
Olive oil
1 clove garlic, chopped

FOR THE CABBAGE
1 tablespoon olive oil
1 onion, cut in large chunks

1 cooking apple, peeled, cored,
halved and sliced
1 green pepper, seeded and sliced
1 red cabbage, shredded
1 teaspoon balsamic vinegar
100 ml (3½ fl oz) red wine
25 g (1 oz) butter
2 star-anise
1 tablespoon fresh chopped chervil
1 teaspoon caster sugar
Salt and freshly ground black pepper
1 tablespoon Greek yoghurt, to serve
Chervil sprigs, to garnish

Pre-heat the oven to gas mark 7, 220°C, 425°F. In a bowl, mix together the marinade ingredients. De-rind and trim the pork pieces and put them in the bowl. Leave to one side.

Cut the potatoes in half and cut as for fantail potatoes. Par-boil in salted, boiling water for 3 minutes. Drain and brush generously with olive oil. Place in an ovenproof dish, with the garlic. Put in the oven and bake for 20 minutes, until they are cooked through, crisp and golden.

For the cabbage, heat the oil in a wok or deep frying-pan. Fry the onion for 3 minutes or until soft. Add the apple and most of the pepper and cook for a further 5 minutes. Add the cabbage, vinegar, wine, butter, star-anise, chervil and sugar. Season with salt and pepper. Stir continuously for a minute. Cover and leave over a gentle heat for 5 minutes.

Fry the pork with the rest of the pepper in the oil and the marinade in a frying-pan for 8 minutes, turning occasionally. Remove from the pan and deglaze the pan with the wine.

To serve, divide the cabbage between two warmed plates and top with a little Greek yoghurt. Set the pork pieces to one side of the cabbage and pour the sauce over each. Garnish with chervil. Serve with the potatoes.

KEVIN WOODFORD

BEST OF BEEF BAKE

Beef in puff-pastry parcels, with béarnaise sauce and patty-pan squashes

Being a national champion at tug-of-war, Angie Benson wanted Kevin to cook up a hearty beef dish that she could serve to her team-mates.

SERVES 2

FOR THE STEAKS
100 g (4 oz) chicken livers
2 shallots, roughly chopped
1 tablespoon chopped fresh parsley
4 button mushrooms, roughly chopped
1 plum tomato, skinned and chopped
1 garlic clove
Brandy
2 tablespoons olive oil
2 x 125 g (4 oz) ready-rolled puff pastry sheets
2 x 150–175 g (5–6 oz) fillet steaks
1 tablespoon mustard
1 egg yolk, beaten
Salt and freshly ground black pepper

FOR THE SAUCE
2 egg yolks
1 tablespoon white wine
75 g (3 oz) unsalted butter, melted
1 tablespoon chopped fresh parsley
1 tablespoon chopped fresh coriander

FOR THE SQUASHES
25 g (1 oz) butter
6 button mushrooms
2 small squashes, quartered and seeded
Salt and freshly ground black pepper

TO SERVE
1 plum tomato, chopped
Dill sprigs

Pre-heat the oven to gas mark 7, 220°C, 425°F. Put the chicken livers, shallots, parsley, mushrooms, tomato, garlic and a splash of brandy into a food processor, season and blend until quite smooth. Transfer the mixture to a hot frying-pan and fry in 1 tablespoon of the oil. Roll out each piece of pastry into a 20 cm (8 in) square. Flatten the steaks to 5 cm (2 in) thick, by beating them with a rolling-pin or meat hammer. Heat the remaining oil in a hot frying-pan and seal the steaks for a minute on each side. Place the steaks in the middle of the pastry

MEAT DISHES

and brush them with mustard. Spoon the chicken-liver mixture on top. Brush the edges of the pastry with beaten egg yolk and fold the pastry to enclose the meat. Brush the pastry with beaten egg yolk, to glaze. Bake for 15 minutes or until the pastry has browned.

To make the béarnaise sauce, whisk the egg yolks in a heatproof bowl over a pan of simmering water (the water must not touch the bottom of the bowl). Add the wine and whisk until the mixture thickens and the whisk leaves a trail. Gradually stir in the melted butter, leaving the sediment behind in the pan, and, finally, the parsley and coriander.

Meanwhile, heat the butter in a frying-pan, add the whole mushrooms and squashes. Season and fry for 4–5 minutes.

To serve, put the pastry parcels on warmed plates and garnish with chopped tomato and dill sprigs. Spoon some sauce on the side and accompany with the squashes and mushrooms.

KEVIN WOODFORD

BONFIRE BONANZA BROTH

Bacon 'Catherine wheels' and bacon and sweetcorn soup

For Bonfire Night, Rachel wanted something to impress her husband, who, she admitted, was the better cook 'which can be incredibly annoying at times', she added.

SERVES 4
FOR THE CATHERINE WHEELS
150 g (5 oz) shortcrust pastry
1 egg, beaten
225 g (8 oz) unsmoked streaky bacon

FOR THE SOUP
50 g (2 oz) butter
1 onion, chopped
2 garlic cloves, crushed
1 vegetable stock cube, dissolved in 900 ml

(1½ pints) boiling water
2 corn on the cob or 100 g (4 oz) tinned or frozen sweetcorn kernels, drained
1 red pepper, seeded and chopped
2 turnips, peeled and chopped
225 g (8 oz) smoked pork sausage, sliced
275 g (10 oz) potatoes, peeled and cubed
1 tablespoon tomato purée
2 tablespoons chopped fresh coriander
Salt and freshly ground black pepper

73

VARIATION Worcestershire sauce
Tabasco sauce   1–2 garlic cloves, crushed
$^1/_2$ teaspoon chilli powder

Pre-heat the oven to gas mark 6, 200°C, 400°F. Roll out the pastry on a floured board into a 25 cm (10 in) by 13 cm (5 in) oblong about 5 mm ($^1/_4$ in) thick and brush with some of the egg. De-rind five rashers of the bacon and lay them on top of the pastry. Roll the pastry into a sausage lengthways, cut it into 1 cm ($^1/_2$ in) slices and brush with the remaining egg. Put on a greased baking sheet and bake for 12–15 minutes, or until golden.

For the soup, melt the butter in a saucepan, add the onion and garlic and cook until soft. Add the stock. Cut the remaining bacon into strips. Cut the kernels from the corn cobs, if using. Add the bacon and corn to the soup, with the red pepper, turnips, sausage, potatoes, tomato purée, coriander and seasoning. Bring to the boil, then simmer for 15–20 minutes, until potatoes are tender.

For a spicier version, add 3 drops of Tabasco, the chilli powder, a splash of Worcestershire sauce and some extra garlic into the pan with the stock and continue recipe as above.

ANNETTE'S AUSSIE ARTICHOKES

Marinated pork medallions with artichoke crisps and soubise sauce

Having returned to Banstead from Australia, Annette Richardson was keen to combine true British cooking with a bit of down under. The finished meal was so delicious, Annette was tempted to stay.

SERVES 2
FOR THE RICE
1 tablespoon olive oil
$1/_2$ onion, chopped
100 g (4 oz) rice
1 garlic clove, crushed
1 tablespoon chopped fresh coriander
1 tablespoon chopped fresh parsley
1 tablespoon chopped fresh dill
400 ml (14 fl oz) chicken stock

FOR THE ARTICHOKE CRISPS
1 tablespoon lemon juice
2 Jerusalem artichokes, peeled
Oil for deep-frying

FOR THE MEDALLIONS
2 tablespoons clear honey
1 tablespoon Dijon mustard

4 tablespoons olive oil
2 parsley sprigs
2 pork chops
Salt and freshly ground black pepper

FOR THE VEGETABLES
$1/_2$ onion, chopped
1 yellow pepper, sliced
50 g (2 oz) mushrooms, sliced
2 tablespoons white wine

FOR THE SAUCE
2 tablespoon double cream
1 egg yolk
Parsley sprigs, to garnish

For the rice, heat the oil in a pan, add the onion and cook for 3 minutes. Add the rice, garlic, herbs and stock. Bring the mixture to the boil and reduce the heat and then cover. Cook thoroughly for 12–15 minutes, until the rice is tender and has absorbed all the liquid.

Add the lemon juice to a bowl of cold water and put in the artichoke slices as you cut them thinly, using a mandolin or sharp knife.

To make the marinade, put the honey, mustard, 2 tablespoons of oil, parsley and seasoning into a bowl and mix well. Trim the bone and fat off the chops to leave the medallion, place the meat in the marinade, turn to coat both sides and leave for at least 5 minutes.

Heat the remaining oil in a pan, add the pork and cook on both sides for 2 minutes. Transfer to grill pan and grill for 4 minutes on each side, until thoroughly cooked.

Add the onion, pepper and mushrooms to the pan in which you cooked the pork and cook for 2 minutes. Add the wine and cook until tender.

To fry the crisps, heat the oil for deep-frying in a wok or deep frying-pan. Drain the artichoke slices and pat dry on kitchen paper. Add them to the hot oil, in batches, if necessary, and cook until crisp and lightly browned. Drain on kitchen paper.

For the sauce, whip the cream until thick and add the egg yolk. Place in a food processor, with 3 tablespoons of the rice and blend together, until smooth.

Divide the remaining rice between two warmed plates. Add the pork, with a spoonful of the soubise sauce on top. Put the pepper and mushroom mixture round the side and garnish with the artichoke crisps and sprigs of parsley.

READY STEADY COOK Tips
Always drop artichoke slices into acidulated water to prevent them from turning brown.

If you can leave the meat in the marinade a little longer, it will help to improve the flavours.

You can make 'crisps' with other vegetables such as aubergine, courgette – or potato!

DESSERTS

READY STEADY COOK 3

LESLEY WATERS

DIVERTING DESSERT SELECTION

Cherry and chocolate baked Alaska, caramelized satsumas and hot cherry sauce and vanilla ice cream

Jan Cooper brought along things she always has hanging around her house at Christmas and wondered if something exciting could come from after-dinner mints and satsumas: it could!

SERVES 10	25 cm (10 in) sponge flan case
FOR THE SATSUMAS	680 g (1 lb 6 oz) jar of pitted cherries in syrup
100 g (4 oz) granulated sugar	2 litres (3^1/$_2$ pints) vanilla ice cream
10 satsumas	100 g (4 oz) chocolate mint wafers
Juice of 1 orange	2 teaspoons arrowroot
100 ml (3^1/$_2$ fl oz) water	2 tablespoons cold water

FOR THE ALASKA AND HOT CHERRIES	TO DECORATE
5 size-3 egg whites	Icing sugar
375 g (13 oz) caster sugar	Mint sprigs

Pre-heat the oven to gas mark 7, 220°C, 425°F. Put the granulated sugar in a heavy-based pan with half the water. Heat gently until the sugar has dissolved. Boil steadily, without stirring, for 10–12 minutes, until the syrup turns to caramel and is golden brown. Add the remaining water (take care to stand back as the pan will hiss). Stir until all the lumps have dissolved and set to one side.

Put the unpeeled satsumas in a bowl, cover with boiling water and set aside.

Whisk the egg whites to stiff peaks and then gradually whisk in 275 g (10 oz) of the caster sugar. Continue whisking until the meringue mixture is very thick and glossy.

Put the flan case on a baking sheet and spoon half of the cherries into the case. Pile half of the ice cream on top of the cherries and

78

soften slightly with a spoon. Break the chocolate mints into pieces and push them into the ice cream. Spread the meringue mixture all over the ice cream, making sure there are no gaps, and then sprinkle over 25 g (1 oz) of caster sugar. Bake for 4–5 minutes, until the meringue is lightly browned. Don't allow it to burn. Dust the baked Alaska with icing sugar and decorate with sprigs of mint.

Put the rest of the cherries, the syrup from the jar and the remaining sugar in a pan. Blend the arrowroot with the water and stir into the cherries and syrup. Bring to the boil, stirring all the time, until thickened.

Drain the satsumas, peel and put in a serving bowl. Add the orange juice to the caramel and pour over the satsumas. Stir well, to coat them in the caramel. Spoon the remaining ice cream into serving bowls and spoon over the hot cherry sauce. Serve the desserts.

L E S L E Y   W A T E R S

KELLY'S SUMMER COLLECTION

Cinnamon meringues, poached peaches, chocolate-dipped brazil nuts and raspberry purée

Kelly Holmes' husband dominated the barbecue over the summer. Kelly had resigned herself just to making the dessert and was looking for something a bit different to steal some of the limelight for herself.

SERVES 2	**FOR THE POACHED PEACHES**
FOR THE MERINGUES	150 g (5 oz) caster sugar
2 egg whites	3 tablespoons white wine
100 g (4 oz) caster sugar	4 tablespoons water
2 teaspoons ground cinnamon	Juice of 2 oranges
	4 cloves
FOR THE CHOCOLATE NUTS	2 peaches, halved and stoned
75 g (3 oz) whole brazil nuts	15 g (1/2 oz) butter
50 g (2 oz) plain chocolate chips	

FOR THE RASPBERRY PURÉE
100 g (4 oz) frozen raspberries
Icing sugar

Mint sprig, to garnish
200 ml (7 floz) ½ x carton crème fraîche

Pre-heat the oven to gas mark 5, 190°C, 375°F. Whisk the egg whites until they hold their shape. While still whisking, add 100 g (4 oz) of the caster sugar, a tablespoon at a time, until the meringue is stiff and shiny. Fold in the cinnamon. Shape the meringues into nine quenelles (egg shapes), using two spoons. Put the quenelles on to baking parchment on a baking sheet and bake for 6–7 minutes, until nicely coloured but still soft in the middle.

Lightly toast the nuts on a baking sheet in the oven for 4–5 minutes as well, turning occasionally.

Melt the chocolate chips in a double boiler and, when melted, dip the whole toasted brazil nuts in it, so that half is covered with the chocolate. Leave to set on baking parchment. With a piping bag drizzle the remaining chocolate over the meringues.

In a small saucepan, put the remaining sugar, the wine and 2 tablespoons of the water and allow the sugar to dissolve.

Add half the orange juice to the sugar syrup, with another 2 tablespoons of water and the cloves. Put the peaches in, flesh-side down, and leave to poach for 8–10 minutes, until softened but still firm in the centre.

Put the frozen raspberries and a tablespoon of icing sugar into a food processor and process to make a purée.

Flood each plate with the raspberry purée. Place a poached peach in the centre of each plate and decorate with the chocolate covered nuts and meringues. Garnish with a sprig of mint and serve with the créme fraîche in a separate dish.

D E S S E R T S

L E S L E Y   W A T E R S

PUT-YOUR-FEET-UP PUDDING

Individual ratafia trifles, ratafia and nectarine *brûlée* and strawberries and cream swirl

At six feet six inches, Matthew Rose towered above Lesley and Fern as he tipped his ingredients on to the counter. It was only a couple of days away from Mother's Day and Matthew wanted to treat mum, Helena, to something special. Helena came along to watch and have a taste.

SERVES 4

FOR THE *BRÛLÉE*
100 g (4 oz) almond ratafias
250 g (9 oz) seedless green grapes
2 oranges
2 nectarines, sliced
250 ml (8 fl oz) double cream
2 tablespoons demerara sugar

FOR THE SAUCE
225 (8 oz) strawberries, hulled
Juice of $\frac{1}{2}$ orange
1 tablespoon icing sugar
200 ml (7 fl oz) crème fraîche
3 tablespoons Greek yoghurt

TO DECORATE
Icing sugar
Cocoa powder

Pre-heat the grill to a medium heat. For the *brûlée*, crumble the ratafias, reserve 2 tablespoons and spread the remainder over the base of an ovenproof, shallow dish. Sprinkle over half the grapes. With a sharp knife, cut the zest and pith off the oranges and slice the flesh. Layer over the grapes in the dish, with the sliced nectarines. Pour over the cream and sprinkle over the sugar. Place under grill for 10–12 minutes, to caramelize the sugar.

Meanwhile, for the trifles, put the reserved ratafias in the base of two wine glasses.

For the swirl, reserve two large whole strawberries and place the rest in a liquidizer or food processor. Add half the orange juice and the icing sugar and purée to form a smooth coulis.

Spoon the remaining orange juice over the ratafias in the wine glasses, add three-quarters of the remaining grapes and half the crème fraîche. Spoon over half the strawberry coulis.

In a bowl, mix the remaining crème fraîche with the yoghurt. Spoon this over one half of a serving plate, spoon the remaining coulis over the other half and, with a fork, swirl the two together to make a pattern. Halve the two remaining strawberries, make a pile of these and the remaining grapes in the centre and sprinkle with icing sugar.

Remove the hot pudding from the grill and sprinkle with a little cocoa powder. Serve the three desserts.

LESLEY WATERS

A TRIFLE DIFFERENT AND EXOTIC FRUIT HOT-POT

Pineapple and ginger meringue trifle and stewed exotic fruit

Chris Dowling could never be bothered to make sweets but, when he goes out, desserts take precedence over all other courses! He needed a quick and simple pudding that he could make at home.

SERVES 6	FOR THE HOT-POT
FOR THE MERINGUE TRIFLE	8 tablespoons granulated sugar
4 size-3 egg whites	300 ml (10 fl oz) water
225 (8 oz) caster sugar	1 cinnamon stick
1 Jamaican ginger cake, cut	1 bay leaf
in 1 cm ($^1/_2$ in) slices	$^1/_2$ lemon, juice and zest
432 g (15 oz) tin of pineapple pieces	$^1/_2$ orange, juice and zest
in natural juice	1 star fruit, sliced widthways
1 orange, peeled and sliced	1 tablespoon white wine
Juice of 1 orange	1 pawpaw, peeled, seeded and sliced
	225 g (8 oz) strawberries, hulled and halved
	Greek yoghurt, to serve (optional)

D E S S E R T S

Pre-heat the oven to gas mark 6, 200°C, 400°F. Put the egg whites in a clean, grease-free bowl and whisk to stiff peaks. Gradually whisk in the caster sugar and continue whisking until the meringue mixture is very thick and glossy.

Lay the slices of ginger cake in the base of a large ovenproof dish and then pour the pineapple pieces and some of the juice from the tin over the cake. Scatter the orange slices and juice of one orange over the pineapple. Spoon the meringue mixture over the top and cover loosely with foil. Bake in the oven for 5 minutes, until the meringue is golden. Remove the foil and bake for a further 10 minutes.

Put the granulated sugar, water, cinnamon, bay leaf and lemon and orange zest in a large pan and simmer for 5 minutes until syrupy. Add the star fruit, wine and juice of the half-orange and half-lemon. Simmer for 2 minutes. Add the pawpaw and strawberries and simmer for 3 minutes.

Spoon the exotic fruit hot-pot into a serving bowl and serve with Greek yoghurt, if you like. Serve the meringue trifle separately.

L E S L E Y   W A T E R S

CHARLOTTE'S CHOCOLATE PASSION

Chocolate roulade with kirsch-flavoured cream, black cherries and a chocolate and cherry sauce

Charlotte confessed that she and her husband both had a sweet tooth and said they would love another way of eating chocolate. She also admitted to having been a bit slack on cooking since the arrival of their new baby – the night before she'd fed her husband just on toast!

SERVES 6–8	300 ml (10 fl oz) double cream
3 eggs	Miniature bottle or 4 tablespoons of kirsch
100 g (4 oz) caster sugar	100 g (4 oz) luxury dark chocolate
50 g (2 oz) plain flour	425 g (15 oz) tin of pitted black cherries
25 g (1 oz) cocoa	

83

TO DECORATE   Mint sprigs
Icing sugar

Pre-heat the oven to gas mark 6, 200°C, 400°F. Break the eggs into a mixing bowl, add the sugar and whisk with an electric whisk, until pale and fluffy. Sift the flour and cocoa together and, with a tablespoon, very gently fold them in, without knocking out the air.

Line a swiss roll tin with baking parchment and pour in the mixture. Gently smooth out to the corners. Bake for about 8–10 minutes, until just firm. Cool in the tin for a few minutes then turn out on a wire rack and leave to cool further.

Whisk the cream until just thick and stir in half the kirsch.

Melt the chocolate in a bowl over a pan of boiling water. Make an icing bag from a triangle of greaseproof paper. Spoon in a tablespoon of melted chocolate, pipe shapes on to a sheet of greaseproof paper and chill.

Stir the remaining kirsch into the melted chocolate, with 2 tablespoons of the cherry juice (add extra if the sauce is too thick). Pour the sauce into a jug and keep warm, to serve with the dessert.

Remove the sponge from the tin on to a work surface. Spread the sponge with the cream. Drain the cherries and spoon on top of the cream. Start rolling it up lengthways, peeling off the paper as you go.

Lift the roulade on to a serving plate and dredge with a little icing sugar. Peel the chocolate shapes off the paper and lay them on top of the roll. Decorate the side of the plate with mint sprigs.

L E S L E Y   W A T E R S

PASSION FOR PINEAPPLE

Pineapple and orange *mille feuilles* and stuffed fresh pineapple

Addicted to puddings and chocolate, Ann Frances from Wakefield brought along her favourite ingredients, with a tub of fromage frais 'to counteract the chocolate'.

SERVES 2	50 g (2 oz) blanched whole almonds
350 g (12 oz) ready-to-roll puff pastry	100 g (4 oz) continental plain chocolate
3 oranges	300 ml (10 fl oz) double cream
4 tablespoons sugar	1 tablespoon icing sugar
1 medium fresh pineapple	200 g (7 oz) light fromage frais or crème
25 g (1 oz) butter	fraîche, to serve

Pre-heat the oven to gas mark 6, 200°C, 400°F. On a lightly floured surface, roll out the puff pastry to a 30 cm (12 in) by 20 cm (8 in) oblong, 5 mm (¼ in) thick. Lift on to a greased baking sheet, prick all over and bake for 8 minutes. When it is golden and risen, remove from the oven and trim off the edges. Then cut the pastry into three widthways and put to one side.

Meanwhile, remove the zest from the oranges. In a small pan, put the orange zest and sugar. Cover with water and leave to simmer over a gentle heat, until the sugar has dissolved.

To prepare the pineapple, cut it lengthways, keeping the leaves intact. Hollow out both sides. Cut half the flesh into cubes, roughly chop the remainder and keep separately to one side.

Heat the butter in a large pan and toast the almonds, until golden. Add the roughly chopped pineapple and heat through. Add the orange and sugar mixture. Mix together and keep warm.

Melt the chocolate in a double boiler. Meanwhile, whip the cream until it holds its shape. Then peel the oranges and slice them.

To assemble, spread one-third of the cream on one piece of the pastry, put half the pineapple cubes and orange slices on the cream and drizzle over 2 tablespoons of the melted chocolate. Put another layer of pastry on top and repeat. Finish with the third layer of pastry and dust with icing sugar.

Spoon the pineapple and nut mixture into one half of the hollowed-out pineapple and drizzle over the remaining chocolate. Serve with the fromage frais or crème fraîche.

KEVIN WOODFORD

LOUISE'S PASSION

Poached meringues with *crème anglaise* and fresh orange

A true pudding-lover, Louise wanted to give Kevin a real challenge, with unusual and exotic fruits, including a couple she'd never even heard of herself until she spotted them in the supermarket!

SERVES 2	1 tablespoon caster sugar
FOR THE MERINGUES	300 ml (10 fl oz) milk
300 ml (10 fl oz) milk	1 grenadillo
Vanilla pod, halved	1 orange
2 eggs whites	1 mango, stoned and chopped finely
100 g (4 oz) caster sugar	10 physalis (Cape gooseberries), husks peeled back
FOR THE *CRÈME ANGLAISE*	2 tablespoons flaked almonds, to decorate
2 egg yolks	

Pour half the milk into a saucepan, heat gently with half the vanilla pod.

Pre-heat the grill to a hot heat. Spread the almonds on a baking tray and brown under the grill for 2 minutes, until golden. Set aside.

Whisk the egg whites until stiff and gradually add the caster sugar, until you have a soft meringue. Warm two tablespoons in hot water and scoop out a spoonful of the egg-white mixture. Mould into an egg-shaped quenelle, using the spoons and drop gently into the

DESSERTS

heated milk. Bring the milk to the boil and cook for 2–3 minutes. Then remove to a plate. Repeat to make a further quenelle.

Meanwhile, make the *crème anglaise* (custard) in a bain-marie. Put the 2 egg yolks, and a tablespoon of caster sugar in a bowl and set the bowl over a saucepan of boiling water. Heat the remaining milk with the other half of the vanilla pod in a pan to just below boiling point. Remove the vanilla pod. Then add the milk to the egg mixture and whisk constantly over the pan of water until slightly thickened. It should thinly coat the back of a wooden spoon.

Cut the grenadillo in half and scoop the soft, seedy centre into the *crème anglaise*. Reserve one half for decoration.

Use the zest of the orange as a garnish and peel the segments.

To serve, spoon the *crème anglaise* on to a plate. Arrange the orange segments and mango around the plate and place the meringues on top. Garnish with the physalis and browned almonds.

KEVIN WOODFORD

GABRIELLA'S PEARS ON A BED OF HOT CHOCOLATE SCONES WITH ZABAGLIONE

Chocolate scones with apple purée, poached pears and zabaglione

Gabriella asked Kevin to create something that would tempt boyfriend John to propose – after ten years of courting!

SERVES 2
FOR THE SCONES
50 g (2 oz) butter
100 g (4 oz) plain flour, sifted
1 tablespoon caster sugar
1 tablespoon chocolate chips

50 ml (2 fl oz) milk

FOR THE PEARS
2 pears, peeled
450 ml (15 fl oz) white wine
4 tablespoons caster sugar

87

READY STEADY COOK 3

FOR THE APPLE PURÉE
5 apples, peeled and quartered
300 ml (10 fl oz) water
1 teaspoon ground cinnamon
1 tablespoon caster sugar

FOR THE ZABAGLIONE
3 yolks
2 tablespoons caster sugar
75 g (3 oz) butter, melted
Lemon juice
Apple slices, sprig of mint, to garnish (optional)

Pre-heat the oven to gas mark 6, 200°C, 400°F. Rub the butter and flour together, until the mixture resembles breadcrumbs. Add the sugar and chocolate chips and enough milk to gather the mixture together, to form a dough. Divide into two equal balls and make each into a 10 cm (4 in) round scone. Place on a greased baking sheet and bake for 10–12 minutes.

Put the pears in a saucepan, with the wine and caster sugar. Bring to the boil and then simmer gently, with the lid on, for 15 minutes. Remove the pears from the wine and hollow out the bottom of each pear, so it will stand up.

Cook the apples in the water, with a pinch of cinnamon and the caster sugar. Bring to the boil and then leave to simmer for 10–12 minutes, until the apples are soft. Beat to a smooth purée over a high heat.

To make the zabaglione, whisk the egg yolks in a bowl over a pan of boiling water for 1 minute. Add the caster sugar and continue to whisk over the heat, until the mixture starts to thicken and turn white in colour. Slowly add the melted butter, whisking constantly. Stir in a squeeze of lemon juice and set aside the zabaglione.

Pre-heat the grill to hot. Place the scones on a plate. Spoon the apple purée on top and then put a pear on the apple. Pour the zabaglione over and grill for 2 minutes. Serve while still warm, garnished with apple slices and a sprig of mint, if you like.

DESSERTS

KEVIN WOODFORD

RACHEL'S RUDE AND RASPBERRY PUDDING

Dried fruit steamed pudding with raspberry cream sauce

With her first wedding anniversary just around the corner, Rachel Williams wanted something 'naughty but nice' to make sure that she and husband Bruce made it to their second anniversary.

SERVES 4
FOR THE PUDDING
50 g (2 oz) mixed dried fruit, e.g. prunes, figs and apricots, chopped
50 g (2 oz) butter, softened
100 g (4 oz) soft light brown sugar
2 eggs, beaten
100 g (4 oz) self-raising flour, sifted

2 tablespoons milk
2 tablespoons golden syrup

FOR THE RASPBERRY CREAM
290 g (10$\frac{1}{2}$ oz) tin of raspberries in apple juice, drained and juice reserved
300 ml (10 fl oz) double cream
Dried fruit, sliced, to garnish (optional)

Soak the dried fruit in the juice from the tin of raspberries.

Mix together the butter and sugar in a bowl, with a wooden spoon, until they have creamed and turned a pale yellow. Beat in the eggs, little by little. If the mixture begins to curdle add a tablespoon of the flour. Once the eggs are fully incorporated, fold in the flour gradually. Add the milk. Stir in the soaked fruit (reserve the juice).

Put the golden syrup into the bottom of a buttered 2-pint, heatproof pudding basin. Spoon the sponge mixture on top, cover with microwave-safe cling film, pierce and microwave for 4 minutes at full power. Leave to stand for 5 minutes.

To make the raspberry sauce, mash the raspberries with a fork. Stir in the double cream. Whisk to thicken the cream.

To serve, invert the sponge on to a plate. Serve with the raspberry sauce. Surround the pudding with slices of dried fruit, if you like.

KEVIN WOODFORD

COPACABANA PUDDING

Kumquat, pineapple and apple crumble with custard

Part-time jazz-singer, Gina Browne, wanted a pudding to tempt her husband Jonathan, whom she met when she went into his shop to buy a pair of trousers.

SERVES 4

FOR THE CRUMBLE
50 g (2 oz) shelled mixed nuts
75 g (3 oz) plain flour
50 g (2 oz) demerara sugar
50 g (2 oz) butter

FOR THE FILLING
25 g (1 oz) butter
100 g (4 oz) kumquats, quartered
1 star fruit, chopped
50 g (2 oz) soft light brown sugar
2 dessert apples, peeled, cored and chopped

150 g (5 oz) fresh pineapple, cut in chunks, or a 200 g (7 oz) tin of pineapple chunks, drained

FOR THE CUSTARD SAUCE
450 ml (15 fl oz) milk
4 eggs
25 g (1 oz) caster sugar
1 passion-fruit, halved

TO DECORATE
Slices of lime
Mint sprigs

Pre-heat the oven to gas mark 7, 220°C, 425°F. Dry-fry the nuts in a frying-pan for 3 minutes, stirring frequently, until golden. Put in a food processor and process until roughly chopped. Add the flour and sugar and mix well. Add the butter and process until the mixture looks like coarse breadcrumbs.

For the filling, melt the butter in a large frying-pan. Add the kumquats and cook for 2 minutes, stirring occasionally. Add the star fruit and sugar and cook for 2 minutes more. Continue to stir occasionally. Add the apples and cook for 2 minutes. Stir in the pineapple chunks and cook for 5 minutes.

Spoon the fruit mixture into four 10 cm (4 in) glass ovenproof ramekin dishes. Top with the crumble and stand on a baking tray.

D E S S E R T S

Bake for 8–10 minutes, until the crumble topping is golden.

Meanwhile, make the custard sauce, by gently heating the milk to just below boiling point in a pan. Put the eggs in a heatproof bowl, place over a pan of boiling water (the water must not touch the bowl) and whisk for 3 minutes. Add the caster sugar and whisk by hand for a further 3 minutes. Slowly pour the hot milk over the eggs and sugar, whisking all the time.

Scoop the pulp and seeds out of the passion-fruit and stir them into the custard. Continue whisking for 5 minutes, until the custard is thick enough to coat the back of a spoon. Taste and add a little more sugar if necessary. Serve the tropical-fruit crumbles with the passion-fruit custard and decorate with slices of lime and sprigs of mint.

K E V I N   W O O D F O R D

BANANADRAMA

Banana and custard baked meringue, banana gratin and banana custard

Despite breaking one of her eggs while tipping out her ingredients, Pat from Preston was stunned when Kevin, one egg down, still managed to create not one, not two but three amazing puddings in just 20 minutes!

SERVES 4–6

FOR THE MERINGUE
1 oblong Madeira cake
Grated zest from 1 lemon and 1 lime
1 banana, sliced
3 tablespoons strawberry jam
200 g (7 oz) caster sugar
150 ml (5 fl oz) white wine
Juice and zest of 1 orange
3 eggs, separated
300 ml (10 fl oz) milk

$^1/_2$ teaspoon vanilla essence

FOR THE GRATIN
2 bananas
25 g (1 oz) butter
1 tablespoon demerara sugar
$^1/_2$ teaspoon grated nutmeg

FOR THE BANANA CUSTARD
1 banana, sliced
Slices of orange, to decorate

91

Pre-heat the oven to gas mark 7, 220°C, 425°F. Slice off a quarter of the cake, put into a food processor and blend to form crumbs; set aside. Slice the remaining cake into fingers and put in an ovenproof pudding dish. Sprinkle over the lemon and lime zest and one banana, sliced. Dot over the jam.

Meanwhile, dissolve 100 g (4 oz) of the sugar in the wine in a saucepan over a low heat, add half of the orange juice and all the zest and pour over the cake in the dish.

To make the custard, put the egg yolks in a bowl and set the bowl over a pan of boiling water. With an electric whisk, whisk until pale. Add 50 g (2 oz) of the sugar in three stages, whisking continuously, until pale, fluffy and thickened. Remove from the heat. Meanwhile, heat the milk to just below boiling and pour into the mixture slowly, whisking continuously. Add the vanilla essence. Pour about half the custard on to the dish.

Whisk the egg whites to stiff peaks and then whisk in the remaining sugar. Pipe or spoon the meringue on to the custard and bake for 6–8 minutes, until browned.

For the gratin, slice the bananas in half lengthways and then slice thinly. Melt the butter in a frying-pan and add the demerara sugar, the remaining orange juice, the nutmeg and the banana. Cook together for 2 minutes and then transfer to a small ovenproof dish. Spoon over most of the remaining custard, reserving about 3 tablespoons. Sprinkle over the reserved cake crumbs and put into the oven for 5 minutes to warm through and brown the topping.

Put the sliced banana into an individual serving dish and add the reserved custard. Garnish with an orange twist. Serve with the other two desserts.

INDEX

A

apple, kumquat and pineapple
crumble with custard 90-1
artichokes
artichoke crisps 75-6
with two dressings and vegetable
hors d'oeuvre with two
dressings 16-17
aubergines 68-9
stuffed with creamy pork, with
saffron rice 69-70
avocado cream 21-2

B

bacon 'Catherine wheels' and bacon
and sweetcorn soup 73-4
banana and custard baked meringue,
banana gratin and banana
custard 91-2
beans
spicy-bean tortillas with cheese and
avocado cream 21-2
see also green beans
béarniase sauce 72-3
beef
goulash with mashed potatoes and
spiced fried bread 66-7
in puff-pastry parcels, with
béarniase sauce and patty-pan
squashes 72-3
beurre manié 59-60
bisque, basil and prawn 34-5
brazil nuts, chocolate dipped 79-80
bread, spiced fried 66-7
broccoli, sesame 61-2
brussels sprouts, shredded 59-60

C

cabbage see red cabbage
carrots à la Parisienne 39
cheese and tomato filo parcels 27-8
cherry and chocolate baked Alaska
and hot cherry sauce and vanilla
ice cream 78-9
chicken
backpackers' feast 48-9
breast stuffed with apricots, pepper
and chicory salad, spicy rice
and cucumber salad 58-9
paella with chicken-stuffed roasted
peppers 46-7
stir-fried chicken noodles served
with chinese-leaf salad with
peanut sauce 51-2
chicory and pepper salad 58-9
chinese-leaf salad with peanut
sauce 51-2
chocolate
passion 83-4
pears on a bed of hot chocolate
scones with zabaglione 87-8
cod
in a creamy sauce, baked in filo
pastry and served with
mushroom sauce 40-1
steaks with aromatic stewed
peppers, tomato and cheese
filo parcels and roasted-
tomato salad 27-8
courgettes
grilled 28-9
rice 45-6
timbales with tomato sauce 18-19
couscous 48-9
cucumber salad 58-9
custard, banana 91-2
custard sauce 90-1

D

duck
  crisp-griddled with savoury rice,
    sweet and sour sauce, stir-fried
    vegetables and 'seaweed'
    55-6
  golden duck legs with parsnip
    sauce, saffron rice and sesame
    broccoli 61-2
dumplings, herby 56-7

F

fennel and potato rösti 25-6
feta toasties with salsa 14-15
filo pastry
  cod in a creamy sauce, baked in
    filo pastry and served with
    mushroom sauce 40-1
  filo roulade 14-15
  tomato and cheese parcels 27-8
fish
  creamy curry with savoury rice and
    spicy green beans 32-3
  medley of fresh fish on a bed of
    chablis and spring onion
    sauce 42-3
fruit, dried steamed pudding with
  raspberry cream sauce 89

G

ginger and pineapple meringue trifle
  and stewed exotic fruit 82-3
gnocchi with tomato sauce,
  semolina 20-1
green beans
  cardamom beans 30-1
  spicy 32-3

H

haddock mousses with white wine
  and cream sauce and baby
  vegetables 38-9
hog's pudding, sliced white with
  warm potato salad and sweet and
  sour red cabbage 64-5
hoummos 48-9

K

kumquats
  kumquat marmalade 53-4
  kumquat, pineapple and apple
    crumble with custard 90-1

L

lamb
  minced lamb kebabs with
    vegetables in wine, spinach
    and orange salad and
    creamed spinach 65-6
  mouthwatering Mediterranean
    magic 68-9
lasagne, spinach and mushroom
  12-13
leeks, orange 56-7
lobster in wine and cream sauce,
  with herby savoury rice 36-7

M

meringues
  cinnamon, poached peaches, and
    iced raspberry cream 79-80
  poached with crème anglaise and
    fresh orange 86-7
mushrooms
  cod baked in filo pastry with

94

INDEX

mushroom sauce 40-1
mushroom and olive salad 22-3
spinach and mushroom lasagne 12-13
mussels, grilled with herby breadcrumbs 31-2

N

nectarine and ratafia *brûlée* 81-2
noodles, stir-fried chicken served with chinese-leaf salad with peanut sauce 51-2

O

olive and mushroom salad 22-3

P

paella
 paella with chicken-stuffed roasted peppers 46-7
 simple paella 34-5
parsnips
 honey-roasted 53-4
 parsnip sauce with golden duck legs 61-2
pasta spirals in creamy seafood and tomato sauce, with grilled mussels with herby breadcrumbs 31-2
peaches, poached 79-80
pears on a bed of hot chocolate scones with zabaglione 87-8
peppers
 aromatic stewed 27-8
 and chicory salad 58-9
 paella with chicken-stuffed roasted peppers 46-7
petits pois and potatoes 28-9
pineapple

and ginger meringue trifle and stewed exotic fruit 82-3
kumquat, pineapple and apple crumble with custard 90-1
and orange *mille feuilles* and stuffed fresh pineapple 85-6
pizzas, tuna with rustic bread and olive and mushroom salad 22-3
plaice fillets, pan-fried, and tartare sauce with grilled courgettes, potatoes and petits pois 28-9
pork
 aubergines stuffed with creamy pork, with saffron rice 69-70
 marinated medallions with artichoke crisps and soubise sauce 75-6
 pot belly pork 70-1
potatoes
 cheese-and-mustard 30-1
 fennel and potato rösti 25-6
 mashed 66-7, 68-9
 and petits pois 28-9
 potato nests 18-19
 warm potato salad 64-5
prawn and basil bisque 34-5

Q

quail, casseroled in red wine, with shredded sprouts and sweet-potato mash 59-60

R

rabbit casserole with herby dumplings and orange leeks 56-7
raspberries
 raspberry cream sauce 89
 raspberry purée 79-80
 ratafia trifles, individual and